PRAISE FOR

HELP! I'M SAVED!

"Each of us are on a journey with God and He is the biggest part of our stories. This book lays out a direct message about how to begin your own journey with God and how to step into deeper union with a loving Father in order to live the life of surrendered freedom He has for you.

Stef Butler; Actor, Director, Writer

If you've ever wanted someone to sit down with you over a cup of coffee and walk through in a very practical and intentional way the foundational steps to faith in Christ, then this book is for you. The way Jen and Megan write is exactly that. The way they share biblical truth and then practical steps is excellent and deeply personal. You will feel as if they are sitting across the table leading, encouraging and guiding you as you continue to build the foundation of faith that influences the rest of your life in the best way.

Aaron Denn,Pastor

When it comes to someone saying YES to Jesus for the first time, many churches in today's culture are satisfied with a simple hand raised in a service and the tally added to our salvation numbers. The truth is, the moment someone crosses that threshold in their journey of faith is a critical window the Church must embrace and strategically plan for! New believers are faced with a myriad of questions, concerns, and are in dire need of guidance, support, and encouragement.

In this book, Jen and Megan clearly identify and clarify many of the above hurdles, and systematically lay out a path of beginning a healthy journey toward becoming a mature Christ follower. This is a must read for anyone new to faith and a powerful tool churches should add to their arsenal toward fulfilling the Great Commission.

Ryan Loffer, Pastor

HELP I'M SAVED

A FIELD GUIDE FOR THOSE NEW TO FAITH

JENNIFER ERVIG &
MEGAN MONTERROSA

New Harbor Press
RAPID CITY, SD

Ervig/New Harbor Press
1601 Mt. Rushmore Rd, Ste 3288
Rapid City, SD 57701
https://NewHarborPress.com

Help! I'm Saved! / Jennifer Ervig. -- 1st ed.
ISBN 978-1-63357-257-7

The authors would like to dedicate this book to all those who desperately want to live for Jesus and just need some friends on the journey. Additional thanks to our endorsers: Erica Parkerson, Stefanie Butler, Aaron Denn and Ryan Loffer - the way you live out your lives for others is a treasure. Also, huge thanks to our cheerleader and editor, Pam Couzin - you always make the rest of us look good. That is your gift.

CONTENTS

PREFACE

With the fluidity of today's world - fluidity meaning the seamless transitioning between our physical and online lives - the need for more fluid and accessible means of rudimentary discipleship has been on my heart. It is a tragedy to have all the angels rejoice at a soul saved and then for the family of God down below to do nothing to help them move forward from this joyous moment in time. Thus, the cover art for this book. I don't want you so excited about a new life in Christ only to feel like you're drowning in all things known and unknown about your future.

So discipled - what do I mean by that? My definition of being discipled is ***gaining knowledge of and/or having the ability to hear from and obey the Holy Spirit on your own to renew your identity in and commitment to your Jesus daily***. This is a daily discovery and process that will continue to occur until the day you leave this earth and join your King in your heavenly home. Why should we be discipled? Because we should not be merely hearers of the word (Jesus) but we should do what He says (James 1:22-24). I heard my pastor, Nik Baumgart, say it this way: "discipleship is action oriented." It is with great joy that I present you with this book to "figuratively hold your hand" as you begin your walk or recommitment to your walk with Christ. In other words, as you begin to be action oriented in your faith.

It is also my great pleasure to introduce you to my friend and co-author, Megan Monterrosa. She is treasured of the Lord and has an incredible gift as a teacher and writer. You can find more writings from her at Pearls and Pursuit as well as Life and Limb Blog.

Some of the content presented to you here is adapted from past blogs or books that we've each written. The rest is all original just for you! You'll find that the chapters will be followed up with coaching questions that you will sit and wrestle with for a bit so feel free to grab a journal and jot down your initial thoughts. Then, maybe even go back and revise after you think it over for a few days.

You'll also see hyperlinks throughout the digital version of the book that will lead you to further content to enrich your learning.

When it comes to references to passages in the bible, we've provided the text as much as possible so you don't have to look it up. However, sometimes the passages are long and a bit much to insert here. When that is the case feel free to google the passage. So if you see John 1:1 and you want to know what it says, simply type "John 1:1" into your search bar and it'll pop up for you.

Lastly, if ever there's a term or thought you don't understand, please feel free to reach out to us through our blogs or social media platforms as well! We're all in this together!

Some things to know:

- Jesus = Christ = The Word = Son of God (these are all the same)
- Stewardship = taking care of what's been given to you and using it well
- Enemy = Satan = The Devil
- Lordship = Supremacy
- Scripture = The Bible = Word of God

AM I SAVED? (JEN)

Introductory Thoughts: On the off chance you haven't given your life to Christ quite yet or for some reason, you're not sure you have, I want to address that right off the top.

Read:

- In the beginning was the Word, and the Word was with God, and the Word was God. (John 1:1)
- [18] Consequently, just as one trespass resulted in condemnation for all people, so also one righteous act resulted in justification and life for all people. [19] For just as through the disobedience of the one man the many were made sinners, so also through the obedience of the one man the many will be made righteous.[20] The law was brought in so that the trespass might increase. But where sin increased, grace increased all the more, [21] so that, just as sin reigned in death, so also grace might reign through righteousness to bring eternal life through Jesus Christ our Lord. (Romans 5:18-21)

- We all, like sheep, have gone astray, each of us has turned to our own way; and the Lord has laid on him the iniquity of us all. (Isaiah 53:6)
- This only have I found: God created mankind upright, but they have gone in search of many schemes (Ecclesiastes 7:29)
- For as in Adam all die, so in Christ all will be made alive. (1 Corinthians 15:22)
- Therefore, just as sin entered the world through one man, and death through sin, and in this way death came to all people, because all sinned. (Romans 5:12)
- fixing our eyes on Jesus, the pioneer and perfecter of faith. For the joy set before him he endured the cross, scorning its shame (Hebrews 12:2)

The whole point of this book is to let you know you're not alone in this life you have in Christ but before you even get there, you must know that you're not alone in life period - why? Because Christ Jesus, another name for Christ, lives and breathes for you! He LITERALLY lives and breathes for you.

What do I mean? God had a plan from the beginning of the creation of the world to bring people into relationship with Him. He purposely created people to think and choose for themselves so that any love or affection they'd feel toward Him would be genuine and of their own free will. The downside to that, is that He saw from the get go that Eve and Adam would make the choices that they did - I mean they're only human after all. But God's great passion and compassion for us would not allow Himself to leave humankind separated from Him.

Therefore, one day in a quaint town you'll come to know as Bethlehem - His son conceived by The Holy Spirit was birthed by the very human and very blessed, Mary. This child grew in wisdom and stature with God and man. He lived a sinless life on purpose, for a purpose - to sacrifice that life in the most gruesome way on our account AND His father's account - to bring us all back into an irrevocable relationship with each other so that we could spend eternity glorying in the presence of God. Why did we need Jesus to sacrifice for us? Well, without getting too far into it, biblical history shows that sins are always atoned for or forgiven by the sacrifice of blood (usually animal). So if a person sins they need a blood sacrifice **to cover their sins**. Jesus lived a life without sin, therefore, he was considered the perfect sacrifice to cover our sins.

It was God's great pleasure to make this happen so that we would not be forever lost and separated from the only one who can love us perfectly. We are even straight up told that He did it for the joy set before Him! (Hebrews 12:2)

When we grasp the reality, sincerity and weight of this gesture, our response is to either turn away or admit that we know without a shadow of a doubt that what has been done on our behalf is true. We admit that we acknowledge it had to happen because we are indeed full of sin and have a tendency to make bad choices. We accept this gift of selfless love and finally, that we would love nothing more than for Jesus to take over our hearts as we give every area of our lives (thought process, desires, dark places, ideologies, hopes, dreams) to the Lordship of Jesus Christ.

With that being said, if you haven't already, pray this prayer with me:

Dear heavenly Father, maker of heaven and earth, and my very being,

I recognize my innate, human flaws. I'm a mess without you.

I believe that you sent your son, Jesus, to die for me and set things right.

I'm forever grateful for that and ask that Jesus would come into my heart, take over my life and wash me clean of every sin I've ever committed or may ever commit again.

I thank you and praise you, in Jesus' name, Amen.

All right, let's get started on this new life of yours ;)

Jen's Coaching Questions:

1. Why do you believe you have "been saved"?
2. What makes you question this process of being saved?
3. What are some lingering questions you have?
4. If you could explain how you feel right now about the decision you've made to live a new life, how would you do it? Could you write that down?

MY IDENTITY IN CHRIST (MEGAN)

Introductory Thoughts: You are a new creation in Christ. When you gave your life to Jesus, your old life of living apart from a relationship with God died and was buried. Your new life in Christ is your new identity. You might be asking, what does following Jesus mean for my lifestyle and who I am as a person?

Read:

- 14 For Christ's love compels us, because we are convinced that one died for all, and therefore all died. 15 And he died for all, that those who live should no longer live for themselves but for him who died for them and was raised again. 16 So from now on we regard no one from a worldly point of view. Though we once regarded Christ in this way, we do so no longer. 17 Therefore, if anyone is in Christ, the new creation has come:[a]

The old has gone, the new is here! (2 Corinthians
5:14-17)

- 3 Praise be to the God and Father of our Lord Jesus
Christ, who has blessed us in the heavenly realms
with every spiritual blessing in Christ. 4 For he
chose us in him before the creation of the world
to be holy and blameless in his sight. In love 5
he[a] predestined us for adoption to sonship[b]
through Jesus Christ, in accordance with his
pleasure and will— 6 to the praise of his glorious
grace, which he has freely given us in the One he
loves. 7 In him we have redemption through his
blood, the forgiveness of sins, in accordance with
the riches of God's grace 8 that he lavished on us.
With all wisdom and understanding, 9 he[c] made
known to us the mystery of his will according to
his good pleasure, which he purposed in Christ,
10 to be put into effect when the times reach
their fulfillment—to bring unity to all things in
heaven and on earth under Christ. 11 In him we
were also chosen,[d] having been predestined
according to the plan of him who works out
everything in conformity with the purpose of
his will, 12 in order that we, who were the first to
put our hope in Christ, might be for the praise
of his glory. 13 And you also were included in
Christ when you heard the message of truth, the

gospel of your salvation. When you believed, you were marked in him with a seal, the promised Holy Spirit, [14] who is a deposit guaranteeing our inheritance until the redemption of those who are God's possession—to the praise of his glory. (Ephesians 1:3-14)

- [1] Now there was a Pharisee, a man named Nicodemus who was a member of the Jewish ruling council. [2] He came to Jesus at night and said, "Rabbi, we know that you are a teacher who has come from God. For no one could perform the signs you are doing if God were not with him." [3] Jesus replied, "Very truly I tell you, no one can see the kingdom of God unless they are born again.[a]" [4] "How can someone be born when they are old?" Nicodemus asked. "Surely they cannot enter a second time into their mother's womb to be born!" [5] Jesus answered, "Very truly I tell you, no one can enter the kingdom of God unless they are born of water and the Spirit. [6] Flesh gives birth to flesh, but the Spirit[b] gives birth to spirit. [7] You should not be surprised at my saying, 'You[c] must be born again.' [8] The wind blows wherever it pleases. You hear its sound, but you cannot tell where it comes from or where it is going. So it is with everyone born of the Spirit." (John 3:1-8)

- I have been crucified with Christ and I no longer live, but Christ lives in me. The life I now live in the body, I live by faith in the Son of God, who loved me and gave himself for me. (Galatians 2:20)

So what does following Jesus mean for you? Good question. The answer may surprise you. It doesn't mean that by tomorrow you need to behave perfectly or you're no longer saved. It means you have a real relationship with Jesus and that every day His love and gentle work in your heart is what changes you from the inside out.

Following Jesus means being secure in the identity of belonging to God and being able to be the you that He really created- the beautiful, unique and very loved individual you are. Because this identity is rooted in Christ and not yourself, it cannot be taken from you, and you will live in a freedom greater than you thought possible.

Every day His love and gentle work in your heart is what changes you from the inside out.

Your identity in Christ:

- Is your new foundation
- Means you have a spiritual inheritance as a son/daughter of God
- Can't be taken from you by any circumstance or situation

We'll look at what these things mean, but first, an important word about your past (or lack thereof):

<u>You are not your past</u>

When we come to Christ, we undoubtedly have come through a lot of stuff. Life is anything but easy and nobody alive hasn't had struggles, failures, difficulties, crises, made choices they regretted, and wished they could do a few things over. I've got 'em, you've got 'em, we've all got 'em- the regrets. The things that hang around weighing us down and making us question whether we really can change or are worthy to be saved at all. This is where you need to remember that God's deep love for you has nothing to do with your actions; it is unconditional. Jesus dying on the cross for you means you get a brand new start as a new person when you come to faith. It cost Him everything to set you free. Anything and everything that existed in your past has been wiped away by the blood of Jesus. Simply put, you are not your past. You have been washed. You have been redeemed. You are born again.

So, who are you now?

You are now a child of God. You even have a new name (Luke 10:20, Revelation 2:17). And this changes everything.

Your New Foundation

Romans 8:15-17 "So you have not received a spirit that makes you fearful slaves. Instead, you received God's Spirit when he adopted you as his own children. Now we call him "Abba, Father." For his Spirit joins with our spirit to affirm that we are God's own children. And since we are his children, we are his heirs. In fact, together with Christ we are heirs of God's glory. But if we are to share his glory, we must also share his suffering."

You've been rescued by God. Your life and your self is no longer defined by the person you were before knowing Christ when you were separated from God by sin. God has adopted you and called you His very own. You belong to Him and you are in fact His child!

The word "Abba' means "Daddy." We all have different memories of our earthly fathers, and some of us never had one or we had ones that mistreated us. But when Scripture is telling you God is your Daddy, it means that He is the perfect father you have always yearned for and have come home to at long last. You can know with certainty He is real, He is for you, He is not angry with you and He delights in you. He is your provider, your support, your strength, and your security. He will never fail you. He knows what you need before you ask (Matthew 6:8).

So your identity is that you are a son or daughter of God. Becoming who you are in Him is a process that will take time, and this "growth" happens the more you get to know Him and you let go of lesser things. God created you in His image and is rejoicing that you have come home. He knows and understands you better than you know yourself.

Your Spiritual Inheritance

As a son or daughter of God, you are an heir! An heir is defined as "a person inheriting and continuing the legacy of a predecessor." In Christ you receive salvation, everything you need for godly living (2 Peter 1:3), abundant promises from God and the guarantee of eternal life and future reward in heaven. Jesus is even preparing your heavenly home where one day you'll spend eternity with Him (John 14:1-4).

Because you are His child you have all the legal rights of a beneficiary. Usually for someone to receive an inheritance, the predecessor needs to pass away first. Jesus did this when He died for you so that when you become His, you are a recipient of present and future promises. Ephesians 1:13-14 explains that you were marked with a seal, the promised Holy Spirit (more about Him in Chapter 12), who is a deposit guaranteeing your inheritance.

You are a person inheriting and continuing the legacy of Jesus.

Your Identity in Christ is Secure and Can't Be Taken Away

The best thing of all is that nothing can ever take you from Jesus- as He put it, quoted in John 10:28, "I give them eternal life, and they shall never perish; no one will snatch them out of my hand."

Jesus even goes beyond eternal life, and promises to help us in the here and now. As Paul wrote in Romans 8:37-39, absolutely NOTHING can ever separate you from the love of Christ- there is no circumstance, person, place, thing, crisis, situation, event, pandemic, job loss, sickness, you name it- nothing can steal away your identity as God's beloved child, heir of salvation and that you belong to Jesus. We are not promised a life without difficulty, the difference is that now you are in Christ and have been brought near to the One who loves you most.

But what about behavior?

Even with all this wonderful news about Jesus giving you a new identity, it's easy to wonder about the expectations of life change. You wonder if having a new identity in Christ means you have to change everything about yourself immediately in an attempt to fit in with other Christians, the people at church, or to please God. It is important for you to know this is not the case. Instead, you can simply focus on growing in your relationship with Jesus and let Him take care of the rest. You don't have to earn your salvation- it has already been purchased with the blood of Christ. Rather, it's about being set free from entanglements that have held you back all your life. As you are cleansed from the sins that once held you, and washed clean by the blood of Christ, you'll start to understand who the "you" is that He created, that bond that has existed since before you were even born. God created only one you, and He is invested in you already and He knows who you really are.

Megan's Coaching Questions:

1. In your own words, what does it mean to be a new creation in Christ?

2. What from your past do you need to release now that the blood of Christ has washed you, so you can live in freedom to be who He created you to be?

3. How does knowing you are adopted by "Daddy" God change your understanding of who He wants to be in your life?

4. How is your identity in Christ different from your old self which has died, now that you are born again?

WHAT'S MY STORY? (MEGAN)

Introductory Thoughts: Did you know you have an amazing story? You really do. Your journey is part of who you are in Christ- every moment has been written and redeemed by God. It's time to learn your story, know it, and go out and share it.

Read:

- They triumphed over him by the blood of the Lamb and by the word of their testimony; they did not love their lives so much as to shrink from death. (Revelation 12:11) [31] What David said was overheard and reported to Saul, and Saul sent for him.
- [32] David said to Saul, "Let no one lose heart on account of this Philistine; your servant will go and fight him." [33] Saul replied, "You are not able to go out against this Philistine and fight him; you are only a young man, and he has been a

> warrior from his youth." [34] But David said to Saul, "Your servant has been keeping his father's sheep. When a lion or a bear came and carried off a sheep from the flock, [35] I went after it, struck it and rescued the sheep from its mouth. When it turned on me, I seized it by its hair, struck it and killed it. [36] Your servant has killed both the lion and the bear; this uncircumcised Philistine will be like one of them, because he has defied the armies of the living God. [37] The Lord who rescued me from the paw of the lion and the paw of the bear will rescue me from the hand of this Philistine." Saul said to David, "Go, and the Lord be with you." (1 Samuel 17:31-37)

Reflecting on your story

You've got a whole life full of unique experiences, struggles, joys, highs and lows that led you to this point. You might have radically come out of some unbelievable things or you might have had a gradual conversion over time. What's important to know is these things are part of who you are and God uses all of them, no matter what. God is a redeemer, which means He is a specialist in turning the most hopeless or unlikely situations into something beautiful and useful.

We use the word "testimony" to describe the particular detailed story you have that is unique to you and is a witness to the miraculous saving power of Christ.

Take some time to think and pray over the details of your life. Draw a timeline of significant events and ask God to open your eyes and show you what you haven't seen before. This will include the good, the bad and the ugly. I encourage you to stay connected to God as you visit painful memories and let Him show you how He is working for your good and is redeeming those difficult experiences.

Your story is part of who God made you to be, and is not in conflict with your new identity in Christ. Remember that God created you to be the you that He planned before you were born. He knew everything that would happen in your past, present and future. Yes, there are sins and hindrances that God will deal with in our lives while at the same time Jesus continues to change us from the inside out. In addition He purifies, prunes and reveals who He called you to be, eagerly waiting for the new you to be revealed.

Over time God will continue shaping you, healing the past, and will be faithful to walk with you through issues in life helping you follow Christ.

Your story is part of who God made you to be, and is not in conflict with your new identity in Christ.

When you begin writing out your testimony, a couple of wonderful things will happen. You'll be full of joy as you start to see the ways God has been moving in your life over the years. You will remember precious pieces of your story that were long forgotten and see the intentional path God has been leading you on. You might even have some aha moments that give you insight into who God made you to be, where He wants you to go next or changes that He wants you to make for the better.

There will be some powerful moments between you and God as you do this.

Your testimony will start to emerge.

Sharing Your Story

You, whose life has been transformed by grace, who has been rescued and forgiven of much by Jesus, don't let the enemy silence you. Share your testimony. We need you to tell your story.

I may not know you personally, but I can say with certainty that someone's life will change when they hear what God has been doing in yours. Your testimony is a unique weapon fashioned by the hand of God that has the power to overcome darkness.

Trouble is, we forget how powerful our stories are or we don't believe they are anything special. They get buried under familiarity and busyness. They get thwarted by fear of speaking out or by comparison. Maybe you've never stopped to consider that yours has been written by God for the specific purpose that people need to hear it.

Your witness is incredibly deadly to the enemy's work in this world. Revelation 12:11 says "and they (followers of Jesus) have defeated him (the devil, the accuser of the people of God) by the blood of the Lamb ***and by their testimony***. And they did not love their lives so much that they were afraid to die (items in parentheses and emphasis mine)."

When you share with others about how Christ has transformed your life, you literally defeat the enemy who wants to keep someone else in the dark about Jesus and who wants to accuse you.

People can argue or disagree with you all day long about faith- but ain't nobody can tell you your story isn't valid. It is your experience, you can speak exactly to what all has happened, and it cannot be disputed. You are an eyewitness with a first-hand account of what God has done.

We can be told the truth a hundred times, but when we hear someone's personal experience with it, suddenly it becomes real to us.

Your story can resonate and build bridges with people who need to encounter God.

Your witness can reach people that mine could not.

Your journey can give hope to someone who has lost all hope.

Your testimony can pummel down barriers straight into someone's heart.

Your firsthand account will validate the truth of Jesus that you are sharing.

Your story can even encourage your own self in times of difficulty, those times when you need to remember your belief in God's faithfulness to be able to move ahead in faith.

When David faced Goliath, his testimony was what gave him the courage to face a formidable enemy, but not as formidable as the God who had rescued him from the lion and the bear. (1 Samuel 17:31-37)

Tell your story. God has written it but you are the message bearer. Let your testimony do what it was designed to do, because someone out there is waiting for the breakthrough in their life that it will bring.

God will open doors and conversations for you to share with others, so it's good stewardship to know your story and let God shape it in your heart. Think of someone you know who needs to hear about God's miracles performed in your life. You don't have to be abrasive or pushy; but have the readiness to testify when the opportunity comes. Don't be silenced by comparison, fear or shame.

You are a miracle and your testimony of Jesus is a threat to the enemy who wants to bring pain and destruction into your life and into the lives of others. You have authority from your own experience that will tell the world all about who God is. Your story will have an impact that others could not. Now go and overcome by the blood of Jesus, the word of your testimony and be sold out to Christ!

Megan's Coaching Questions:

1. Have you taken time yet to think and pray over your life and write your testimony?

2. What is powerful about what God has done in your life to bring you to Jesus? How can this help others?

3. Why does God say that your testimony overcomes the enemy? How does this happen?

HE CAN HAVE IT ALL (MEGAN)

Introductory Thoughts: As you begin to process your new faith, consider this truth: the more you give up, the more you go up.

Following Jesus is about so much more than simply a one-time prayer. Placing your faith in Christ is the best decision you will ever make and we rejoice with you over this decision. But that's just the beginning. The implications for your life and how you move forward can be summed up in one word: surrender.

Read:

- Then Jesus said to his disciples, [24] "Whoever wants to be my disciple must deny themselves and take up their cross and follow me. [25] For whoever wants to save their life[a] will lose it, but whoever loses their life for me will find it. [26] What good will it be for someone to gain the whole world, yet forfeit their soul? Or what can anyone give in exchange for their soul? (Matthew 16:24-26)

- I have been crucified with Christ and I no longer live, but Christ lives in me. The life I now live in the body, I live by faith in the Son of God, who loved me and gave himself for me.(Galatians 2:20)
- [27] My sheep listen to my voice; I know them, and they follow me. [28] I give them eternal life, and they shall never perish; no one will snatch them out of my hand. (John 10:27-28)

Surrender can be a scary and intense word. It might conjure up images of a person losing a battle and being led away in chains by an enemy army captain. But in God's reality, because of Jesus, surrender equals freedom. It's more like shaking off chains that once held you and experiencing freedom from bondage. Jesus has unlocked the chains, but in your willing surrender you are giving Him permission to remove them. As Jesus put it, when you "lose your life" for His sake, you actually find it (Matthew 16:24-26).

surrender equals freedom.

You willingly let Jesus have every part of you, and in return you get to experience the life He has for you, living in abundant joy. God is a giver, not a taker. He does not force you into submission. He pursued you and sent Jesus to die for you because of His great love and His concern for your welfare and salvation. Because He doesn't use force, it's up to you to decide how far you will pursue your relationship with Him by letting go of your old life and giving every last area of it to the Lordship of Jesus.

This does not mean it's going to be touchy feely all the time, and it certainly is not easy. There will be times when you need to make concrete decisions as a Christ follower to make the right choice- even when difficult- and know that God will meet you there and give you the grace you need to persevere.

Trusting Jesus

Surrender really begins with trusting Jesus, which you've demonstrated by placing your faith in Him. The best way to trust Him more is to know Him. Trust is built over time and in a healthy relationship. With each new day, taking time to spend in prayer and reading about Jesus in Scripture will help you get to know Him.

Every Area

So what does giving every area of your life to Jesus look like on a daily basis? It means you are no longer living for the pursuit of self. It means you make choices out of your earnest desire to be like Jesus and follow His teaching. It means every part of you is being renewed day by day. It's a beautiful and ongoing process which happens over time. You withhold no part and truly give it all to Christ, trusting Him for every next step you take.

In his letter written to the Galatians (an early church), the apostle Paul wrote "I have been crucified with Christ and I no longer live, but Christ lives in me. The life I now live in the body, I live by faith in the Son of God, who loved me and gave himself for me."

Water Baptism

Being "crucified with Christ" means your old life is dead and gone. It was nailed to the cross and you've experienced being born again into new life. This is amazing news! It's time to make a public declaration of your faith in Christ through water baptism.

Being baptized in water is an important step in your journey and should happen as soon as possible after inviting Jesus into your life. The after is important as some faiths baptize infants. While baptizing infants is not a sin, the point of baptizing is not being realized in such a scenario.

Being baptized is a powerful symbol of what has taken place in you spiritually which is why it's such an incredible experience.

When you go under the water, it's symbolic of your old life dying and being buried, and when you come up out of the water it is a celebration of your brand new life as you are "born again". A child who has not made their own decision to give their life to Christ can also not make their own decision to go public with such a choice via baptism.

Water Baptism is very important as it demonstrates your public statement of faith. It's common for people to invite their families and friends to watch their baptism as they are making their faith known and sharing how important it is to them.

You can be baptized with water pretty much anywhere you have a body of water. Churches typically have a baptism tank or inflatable pool for indoor use; you can also be baptized in lakes, rivers, swimming pools, you name it.

<u>Megan's Coaching Questions:</u>

1. What does it mean in your personal life to surrender everything to Jesus?

2. Why does surrender equal freedom for the Christ follower?

3. Do you have a fellow Christian or Pastor who would baptize you?

4. How can you take steps today towards getting water baptized?

HOW TO PRAY (JEN)

Introductory Thoughts: Do you feel like praying is hard or at least hard to grasp?- It can certainly be intimidating. Do you even believe you really know what praying is? When I was first a Christ follower, I felt I stunk at it. Honestly, even sometimes today, I never know what to say. So I just talk to God a lot and ask that He be glorified (recognized and acknowledged as supreme) in whatever the situation is. I'm always jealous of those who seem so eloquent in how they speak to our King. Thank God that we don't have to be conversational experts.

Read:

- The eyes of the Lord are on the righteous, and his ears are attentive to their cry (Psalms 34:15)
- Give ear, our God, and hear; open your eyes and see the desolation of the city that bears your Name. We do not make requests of you because we are righteous, but because of your great mercy. (Daniel 9:18)

- This is the confidence we have in approaching God: that if we ask anything according to his will, he hears us. (1John 5:14)
- Therefore confess your sins to each other and pray for each other so that you may be healed. The prayer of a righteous person is powerful and effective. (James 5:16)

So how do you pray? You just pray. Share your heart with God. That's it. You just talk. You just listen. Prayer is just conversation - heavenly conversation. Honestly, if you stink at praying or feel you do, it's probably all in your head for the most part. I mean, I suppose it's true that some people stink at conversation. Prayer is conversation and conversation takes skill. Well, good conversation takes skill and if you're reading this, it's because you wish to be good at your conversation skills with the love of your life, Jesus.

However, truly good conversation, especially with Jesus, is just taking the focus off yourself and placing it on the other person. No need for eloquent speech or thoughts. But if practical tips are what you're looking for, let's see what we can do.

So I searched up (as my kid used to say) how to be skilled at conversation and this popped up:

Talk slowly. Typically good talkers don't rush into a conversation.

Hold more eye contact. Most people keep eye contact about 2/3 of the time or less when they talk.

Notice the details. How are you feeling? What do you sense is coming from the heart of the other person?

Give unique compliments. People love compliments.

Express your emotion. Are you frustrated? Overjoyed? Don't keep that to yourself.

Offer interesting insights. Share your thoughts and ideas.

Use the best words. This one is interesting isn't it? I'd like to think that for prayer, it means praying the scriptures? Did you know you could do that? I mean the best words surely come from the bible, right? Take James 1:22 for example - you could pray, "Lord, help me be a doer of your word and not only a hearer so that I deceive myself"

Okay, so let's see how we can translate this to our conversational skills with Jesus:

Talk slowly. I don't think this one matters so much. God can listen to you at any speed. If you have something to say, go ahead and spew it out.

Hold more eye contact. Tough to do when we can't tangibly see God. I think for prayer this could mean having a posture of staying focused on the one you're speaking with or praying to. Don't let yourself be distracted by every squirrel that runs by. Have you ever heard the admonition to be where you're at? Show respect for God by being attentive to him and your time with him. Don't be half hearted in your prayer time.

Notice the details. When you're conversing with a person this means to notice their tone of voice or body language. When you're conversing with God, it means to notice those things when reading His word or to be sensitive to the Holy Spirit while you're praying. Who is the Holy Spirit? More on that in a chapter ahead - feel free to come back to this chapter and process more after you find out.

When you notice the details, the other person sees that you genuinely care about what's taking place between the both of you.

Give unique compliments. Give them to the one to whom you love and praise with the kind of praise that he'd only hear from you and the way that you can convey it.

Express your emotions. We connect through emotion. It's one of the benefits that emotions provide.

**pro tip: Read the Psalms, which is a book of prayers, when you're emotional and don't know how to pray. As you read the Psalms you can imagine yourself offering those words up to God in prayer. This is called praying the scriptures and it's powerful.*

Offer interesting insights. God knows what you're thinking and delights in your creative ideas and input, but He wants to hear you express it. Indulge him.

Use the best words. When talking with people, this means to improve our vocabulary. I believe when it comes to prayer it means to memorize Scripture and pray the Scriptures. The Bible is the best written piece of work in existence so use it.

So, do you know how to pray? Are you equipped? If you can think, speak, and reflect, the answer is yes. Sure, use the skills above and cultivate them- but honestly praying is the best form of conversation because all you really have to do is open your heart and God will do the rest.

Jen's Coaching Questions:

1. Why do we sometimes feel like we don't know how to pray?

2. What is it like when you feel like conversation is flowing well with your prayer life? What gets you there?

3. How would you explain your conversations with God to someone who has never prayed?

HOW TO READ THE BIBLE AND MEMORIZE IT (JEN)

Introductory Thoughts: Reading the bible already sounds daunting but I want you to memorize it too. You're thinking I'm nuts, right? Well, maybe not all of it, but I promise you will be surprised what you can do after reading this and putting it into practice. But, honestly, just reading the bible in an effective way, will help you immensely so let's start there.

Read:

- In the beginning was the Word, and the Word was with God, and the Word was God. (John 1:1)
- I have hidden your word in my heart that I might not sin against you. (Psalms 119:11)
- Fix these words of mine in your hearts and minds; tie them as symbols on your hands and bind them on your foreheads. (Deuteronomy 11:18)

- Let the message of Christ dwell among you richly as you teach and admonish one another with all wisdom through psalms, hymns, and songs from the Spirit, singing to God with gratitude in your hearts. (Colossians 3:16)
- I desire to do your will, my God; your law is within my heart. (Psalms 40:8)

Where to Start?

If you're new to bible reading, it's always a good idea to start with what we call The New Testament. You'll find it just over half way through your physical bible or you can always use a bible reading app like YouVersion (find it in your play store) and click on any book of the bible as it will take you right there. Yay, technology!

The New Testament starts with the book, Matthew, and ends with Revelation. You can definitely read straight through Matthew to Revelation but many advise starting with the book of John because he has a way of giving the new believer a beautiful picture of Jesus and His life. In this case, you'd read John, then back up three books to resume with Matthew, then when you get back to John, skip it and head to Acts, then continue on from there.

Why start with the New Testament? Because this testament or covenant is for you. A covenant is an agreement between you and God. The New Testament of the bible explains the terms and conditions of your agreement and relationship with God.

The Old Testament is a historical account of Israel's covenant with God. Israel is just a country of people that God chose to have relationship with in antiquity to eventually bring relationship between Him and all the world. It holds value for all of us as fascinating history as well as revealing who God is and the doctrine of God. However, it is important to read it in light of our own covenant so that we're not confused about our place in the story. Therefore, it is always a good idea to read the New Testament first and use it to help us navigate and apply the Old Testament to who we are today.

Okay now what?

Before you start any chapter of the Bible, do a google search to get a little background information on the book you're about to read. So, if I'm gonna read the book of John I'd google "John Summary". You're looking for information on who wrote the book of John and why. This holds true for any book you read. If you want to read the book of Psalms, google "Psalms Summary" to see who wrote the book of Psalms and why. If you're lucky enough to own a study bible, these summaries will already be printed for you at the beginning of each book. Doing this gives you the context you need to decipher what you're about to read.

By doing this, you'll also discover that the bible is written in different genres of literature. Some of the bible is written as poetry and is intended to make you feel, to stop and think. Some is written as a historical account of events, some are letters from church leaders to churches, and some are prophecies about the future.

Lectio Divina

According to wiki, Lectio Divina, is a traditional monastic practice of scriptural reading, meditation and prayer intended to promote communion with God and to increase the knowledge of God's word. It can be a very helpful way of letting God's word get into you as you get into God's word. When we use lectio divina to read God's word, we choose a passage about six to eight verses long and go through the following process:

Let God's word get into you and you get into God's word.

Quiet ourselves: We quiet our hearts and minds and commit to being with God as a person in the moment ready to receive from Him and give to Him.

Read: We read the passage once or twice looking for keywords that strike us - for some reason the word(s) will jump out at us as important, they resonate with us for some reason. Or maybe they cause us to grimace or be resistant!

Read again: Read the passage again then ask yourself, "what area in my life needed to hear this today?" or "where am I in this story?"

Respond: Respond to God. Is God inviting us to do something through what we just read? Are we challenged? Are we tortured or mad about what we just read? Convicted by our sin? Lay out all your feelings, commitments and thoughts before God in prayer.

Rest: Finally, we read the passage one last time, just resting in who God is. Maybe we've just been encouraged by what we've read or we've had a battle of wits, or an out and out emotional brawl with God over what we just read. No matter what, we will read it one more time and just rest in His love for us and accept His peace.

You don't have to use Lectio Divina every time you read the bible. I know my normal routine is to actually read about 4ish chapters a day so I can read the whole bible in a year. However, in addition to that I like to occasionally pick out six to eight verses and use the practice of Lectio Divina.

The important thing is that you read the Bible everyday even if it's one verse. You can read through the whole Bible in a year by reading four chapters a day or you use Lectio Divina to just really hone in on a few verses at a time. It does not matter how you read the Bible or how much you read as long as you are in the Bible every single day. That is the most important thing.

Memorizing the Bible:

After practicing Lectio Divina, you may want to single out a particular verse/scripture or two and commit it to memory. You can do this by writing it down on a post-it note or card and placing it on your bathroom mirror, dash of your car, or TV remote. Then, every time you use the restroom, jump in your car to go somewhere or switch on Netflix, you can read the verse outloud three times. I say out loud because it uses both your reading and auditory learning. Then, close your eyes and try to recite it from memory. If you can't recite it verbatim, don't worry. Just keep circling through the process above and one day you'll surprise yourself.

Once you have one down, pick a new verse and do it again. Then, begin a stack of all your old post-it notes to quiz yourself on from time to time.

Why memorize scripture?

Good question! Because when we memorize something it becomes part of us. Did you know that John tells us that in the beginning was the word/bible and the word/bible was with God and WAS God?! That means when the bible becomes part of us, God and Jesus are becoming part of us.

When the bible becomes part of us, God and Jesus are becoming part of us.

This is valuable when we're overcome with emotions or facing hard circumstances- in these moments, the things we've memorized just seem to come to mind by the power of the Holy Spirit comforting and encouraging us just when we need it.

This is also valuable when we're trying to tell others about Jesus. Again, the right words that we've already put the work in memorizing just seem to come to mind when we need them.

Additionally, memorizing the bible is very effective for prayer life. Sometimes I don't have the words to pray because I'm emotionally or physically tired and drained. What better way to pray for the will of God than to recite His word to Him?

I should mention, you don't have to memorize the bible to "pray" it. You can simply read the bible and offer up what you're reading as a prayer. Maybe as I'm reading about Paul or David I'd pray "Lord, strengthen me like you did Paul or David" or David's exact words as he says in Psalms, "Lord, create in me a clean heart and renew a right spirit within me." (Psalm 51).

Reading the bible and memorizing it is so valuable to the follower of Christ.

Jen's Coaching Questions:

1. Do you like to read? Why or why not? If you don't like reading, would it stop you from reading the bible?

2. If you've ever read the bible before, where would you tend to get hung up? What was your favorite part?

3. This isn't a question but I just want to encourage you to get a bible dictionary. It's a helpful tool to have around as you read the bible.

WHAT IS WORSHIP? (MEGAN)

Introductory Thoughts: God, in His goodness, really loves you and deeply desires to be with you. Worship is anything you do in response to your desire to be with Him. It can be anything we do with the attitude of "I want to do this well because I love God" or even thinking about Him while doing other things (like chores, working out, going for walks, working...etc.).

Read:

- [1]Now Jesus learned that the Pharisees had heard that he was gaining and baptizing more disciples than John— [2] although in fact it was not Jesus who baptized, but his disciples. [3] So he left Judea and went back once more to Galilee. [4] Now he had to go through Samaria. [5] So he came to a town in Samaria called Sychar, near the plot of ground Jacob had given to his son Joseph. [6] Jacob's well

was there, and Jesus, tired as he was from the
journey, sat down by the well. It was about noon.
7 When a Samaritan woman came to draw water,
Jesus said to her, "Will you give me a drink?" 8 (His
disciples had gone into the town to buy food.) 9
The Samaritan woman said to him, "You are a
Jew and I am a Samaritan woman. How can you
ask me for a drink?" (For Jews do not associate
with Samaritans.[a]) 10 Jesus answered her, "If you
knew the gift of God and who it is that asks you
for a drink, you would have asked him and he
would have given you living water." 11 "Sir," the
woman said, "you have nothing to draw with and
the well is deep. Where can you get this living
water? 12 Are you greater than our father Jacob,
who gave us the well and drank from it himself,
as did also his sons and his livestock?" 13 Jesus
answered, "Everyone who drinks this water will
be thirsty again, 14 but whoever drinks the water
I give them will never thirst. Indeed, the water I
give them will become in them a spring of water
welling up to eternal life." 15 The woman said to
him, "Sir, give me this water so that I won't get
thirsty and have to keep coming here to draw
water." 16 He told her, "Go, call your husband and
come back." 17 "I have no husband," she replied.
Jesus said to her, "You are right when you say

you have no husband. 18 The fact is, you have had
five husbands, and the man you now have is not
your husband. What you have just said is quite
true." 19 "Sir," the woman said, "I can see that
you are a prophet. 20 Our ancestors worshiped
on this mountain, but you Jews claim that the
place where we must worship is in Jerusalem."
21 "Woman," Jesus replied, "believe me, a time
is coming when you will worship the Father
neither on this mountain nor in Jerusalem. 22 You
Samaritans worship what you do not know; we
worship what we do know, for salvation is from
the Jews. 23 Yet a time is coming and has now
come when the true worshipers will worship
the Father in the Spirit and in truth, for they are
the kind of worshipers the Father seeks. 24 God
is spirit, and his worshipers must worship in the
Spirit and in truth." (John 4:1-24)

- Therefore, I urge you, brothers and sisters, in view of God's mercy, to offer your bodies as a living sacrifice, holy and pleasing to God—this is your true and proper worship.(Romans 12:1)
- 37 When he came near the place where the road
goes down the Mount of Olives, the whole
crowd of disciples began joyfully to praise God
in loud voices for all the miracles they had seen:
38 "Blessed is the king who comes in the name

> of the Lord! Peace in heaven and glory in the highest!" [39] Some of the Pharisees in the crowd said to Jesus, "Teacher, rebuke your disciples!" [40] "I tell you," he replied, "if they keep quiet, the stones will cry out." (Luke 19:37-40)

Worship is any act which comes from our spirit showing reverence, love and devotion to God. Worship takes many forms: singing, praising, humbling ourselves before Him, thankfulness, praying, surrendering, obedience, giving, simply sitting in the presence of God, and even serving and loving others. In truth, our whole lives are to be lived as an expression of worship. Even the smallest thing when done or given in a true spirit of worship moves the heart of God (Luke 21:1-4).

God, in His goodness, really loves you and deeply desires to be with you. He created you to worship. If you struggle with knowing your purpose, you can know with certainty you were created to worship and enjoy the Lord.

If you struggle with knowing your purpose, you can know with certainty you were created to worship and enjoy the Lord.

Worship begins in the heart. God deserves worship without question, but He desires that we do so with a willing heart of authenticity. It should always be a result of a heart that loves Jesus and earnestly desires to show Him love using what He gave you. Worship is what we give back to God. Not only does worship give to God what he should have and deserves, it also is a meaningful and beautiful experience for the worshiper. One day, in Heaven, we will worship Him for eternity and never stop.

Here is a practical list of what worship can look like in the life of a believer:

- Corporate worship: when we meet with other believers and sing to God, like in a church gathering or with family and friends.

- Giving tithes and offerings: any giving we do with the right motive is an act of worship.

- Personal worship: when you're alone and you spend time with God singing, praying, and being with Him.

- Obedience: obedience requires our trust in whom we're obeying (God) and is motivated by a heart that loves whom we obey.

- Loving others as Christ loves us: Jesus calls us to love others and is our example. Loving others should define our lives; when we love people we honor and love the God who created them in His image and demonstrates that we are His children (Matthew 5:43-48).

Worship brings us into God's presence

Worship brings us into the presence of God and ignites the fire in our hearts for more of Him. Worship redirects our thoughts, emotions and intentions when they most desperately need to be redirected. As human beings we are prone to forgetting God, especially when we are suffering, under stress and with our overly busy schedules. But when we stop and focus on praising God, suddenly everything changes.

We enter God's presence when we let go of distractions and choose to worship. Sometimes you might be on your knees with your head bowed in adoration. Other times you might jump for joy and shout. It might even mean simply stopping to thank God for what He is doing in any given moment. Worship might be responding to a prompting of the Holy Spirit to be generous in some way. Keep an open mind and heart and never hesitate to let worship pour out of your soul to express your love for God; each time you do so you're going deeper into His presence.

Worship is a choice

Jesus came into the city of Jerusalem shortly before he gave His life on the cross. When he entered the city, people were joyfully shouting and praising God, celebrating what they'd seen God do and witnessing the coming of the Savior. Some of the religious leaders got super upset and tried to make Jesus silence them, but He said "I tell you...if they keep quiet, the stones will cry out." (Luke 19:40) Did you know it's possible for rocks to sing to Jesus? What Jesus was saying here is that He will be worshiped no matter what, even if the very rocks have to be the ones to do it. Creation itself will even respond to worship Him if people refuse. He is that incredible, beautiful and worthy as the Son of God.

Before I lose you or your mind trails off to think about the Rolling Stones, just think of it this way: it's an incredible calling to be chosen by almighty God to be the primary being giving Him praise.

God would rather hear your voice and see your life praising Him than anything else. Even if it doesn't sound great, even if you are uncertain about whether it's good enough- know that it is precious to God because of your heart. One sincere utterance of adoration from you means more to God than a thousand hollow performances.

Worship brings freedom

One of my favorite preachers is fond of saying, "I've never seen anyone who knows how to worship stay bound." I heard this several years ago and have lost count of the number of times it has come to my rescue. Worship has never failed to shatter the limitations on my heart and mind, setting me free. If you are looking for a breakthrough, *you need to worship.*

Why is worship such a powerful strategy for breakthrough? In His presence, chains break, burdens lift and the joy of the Lord gives us strength.

Where the spirit of the Lord is, there is freedom (2 Corinthians 3:17).

Go ahead and make an intentional effort to worship God every place you find yourself. When at home, get the family involved. Turn up the most inspiring worship music you can find and go for it. Be like David in the Bible who was "undignified" in his love for God when he worshiped with all his might (2 Samuel 6:14-23). Refuse to hold back and intentionally engage your whole heart with God. Make worship your top priority, as if your breakthrough depends on it- because it does.

Jesus wants to give you a garment of praise instead of a spirit of despair (Isaiah 61:3).

Worship is a powerful event no matter what form it takes. As David said, "Better is one day in your courts than a thousand elsewhere." (Psalm 84:10) When you express your love and devotion to the Lord through your life and acts of worship you're pleasing to God and you'll find your own breakthrough there too.

Megan's coaching questions:

1. Of all the ways to worship listed here, which one appeals to you the most?

2. What other ways can you think of to express your love for God in worship?

3. What is one type of worship you will intentionally add to your life this week?

SO GENEROUS (JEN)

Introductory Thoughts: Oh no a post on giving! Is that what Christianity is about- getting my money? I promise it's not! Although I wouldn't describe a life with Jesus as "religious" since religion is really just a set of practices or behaviors. There are a few things such as being baptized, taking communion or paying tithes that we DO do in a religious way and for good reason! Haha! Here...let me explain.

Read:

- Bring the whole tithe into the storehouse, that there may be food in my house. Test me in this," says the Lord Almighty, "and see if I will not throw open the floodgates of heaven and pour out so much blessing that there will not be room enough to store it. (Malachi 3:10)
- 1 When you have entered the land the Lord your God is giving you as an inheritance and have taken possession of it and settled in it, 2 take

some of the firstfruits of all that you produce
from the soil of the land the Lord your God is
giving you and put them in a basket. Then go
to the place the Lord your God will choose as a
dwelling for his Name 3 and say to the priest in
office at the time, "I declare today to the Lord
your God that I have come to the land the Lord
swore to our ancestors to give us." 4 The priest
shall take the basket from your hands and set it
down in front of the altar of the Lord your God.
5 Then you shall declare before the Lord your
God: "My father was a wandering Aramean, and
he went down into Egypt with a few people and
lived there and became a great nation, powerful
and numerous. 6 But the Egyptians mistreated us
and made us suffer, subjecting us to harsh labor.
7 Then we cried out to the Lord, the God of our
ancestors, and the Lord heard our voice and saw
our misery, toil and oppression. 8 So the Lord
brought us out of Egypt with a mighty hand and
an outstretched arm, with great terror and with
signs and wonders. 9 He brought us to this place
and gave us this land, a land flowing with milk
and honey; 10 and now I bring the firstfruits of
the soil that you, Lord, have given me." Place the
basket before the Lord your God and bow down
before him. 11 Then you and the Levites and the

foreigners residing among you shall rejoice in all
the good things the Lord your God has given to
you and your household. When you have finished
setting aside a tenth of all your produce in the
third year, the year of the tithe, you shall give it
to the Levite, the foreigner, the fatherless and the
widow, so that they may eat in your towns and
be satisfied. [13] Then say to the Lord your God: "I
have removed from my house the sacred portion
and have given it to the Levite, the foreigner, the
fatherless and the widow, according to all you
commanded. I have not turned aside from your
commands nor have I forgotten any of them. [14] I
have not eaten any of the sacred portion while I
was in mourning, nor have I removed any of it
while I was unclean, nor have I offered any of
it to the dead. I have obeyed the Lord my God;
I have done everything you commanded me.
[15] Look down from heaven, your holy dwelling
place, and bless your people Israel and the land
you have given us as you promised on oath to our
ancestors, a land flowing with milk and honey."
The Lord your God commands you this day to
follow these decrees and laws; carefully observe
them with all your heart and with all your soul. [17]
You have declared this day that the Lord is your
God and that you will walk in obedience to him,

that you will keep his decrees, commands and laws—that you will listen to him. [18] And the Lord has declared this day that you are his people, his treasured possession as he promised, and that you are to keep all his commands. [19] He has declared that he will set you in praise, fame and honor high above all the nations he has made and that you will be a people holy to the Lord your God, as he promised. (Deuteronomy 26)

- You shall remember the LORD your God, for it is He who gives you power to get wealth, that He may establish His covenant which He swore to your ancestors, as it is to this day." (Deuteronomy 8:18)
- [20] where our forerunner, Jesus, has entered on our behalf. He has become a high priest forever, in the order of Melchizedek. 7 [1]This Melchizedek was king of Salem and priest of God Most High. He met Abraham returning from the defeat of the kings and blessed him, [2] and Abraham gave him a tenth of everything. First, the name Melchizedek means "king of righteousness"; then also, "king of Salem" means "king of peace." [3] Without father or mother, without genealogy, without beginning of days or end of life, resembling the Son of God, he remains a priest forever. [4] Just think how great he was: Even the patriarch Abraham

> gave him a tenth of the plunder! [5] Now the law requires the descendants of Levi who become priests to collect a tenth from the people—that is, from their fellow Israelites—even though they also are descended from Abraham. [6] This man, however, did not trace his descent from Levi, yet he collected a tenth from Abraham and blessed him who had the promises. [7] And without doubt the lesser is blessed by the greater. [8] In the one case, the tenth is collected by people who die; but in the other case, by him who is declared to be living. (Hebrews 6:20 -7:1-8)

First, what is tithing? Tithing is giving the first 10% of all money you make to your local church so that the work of God can carry on in the community that your church serves. We do this because God asks us to and all we have monetarily and otherwise belongs to Him because we belong to Him. Not only do we belong to Him but we were created by Him for His purpose so it only makes sense that all that we have comes from Him and is to be stewarded or cared for and used well by us.

Additionally, it should be noted that the bible approaches tithing under the Old Covenant. What is a biblical covenant? It is an agreement for relationship between you and God. A whole separate chapter could be written on what I mean by that but for now, in a nutshell - The Old Covenant was for the Israelites. And the New Covenant was written for all Christ followers for all of time. You may have also heard the covenants referred to as testaments. At any rate, back to our conversation, I believe that you and I are under the New Covenant which may lead one to think we are not required to tithe.

I include a chapter on tithing because I've seen the principles around it play out in my life again and again in a positive way. Take the book of Proverbs for example - although an Old Covenant book, and considered a book of wisdom, much of it is beneficial for us today as general life principles. My take on tithing follows the same vein. I want to make it clear that no matter how much or what you decide to give, it should come out of a heart of generosity and obedience to what you feel The Lord is asking you to do.

Additionally, Hebrews 6:20-7:1-8, in the New Testament, shows us that Jesus has become High Priest forever according to the order of Melchizedek. As High Priest, Jesus now receives the tithes and blesses from the tither. Through this we may come to understand that tithing is very much a part of the New Covenant.

All that being said, even if you agree tithing is for new covenant believers as well, giving a first percentage of our hard earned money to the work of Jesus can be a difficult thing to understand and do. It's my firm belief that when it comes to following Jesus, sometimes understanding can wait but obedience can not. Why? Because obedience proves your level of faith. Obedience demonstrates your trust in Jesus.

Understanding can wait but obedience can not.

Some people tithe on monetary gifts they receive like birthday money as well as what they earn. Some tithe on what they make **before** taxes are taken out and some tithe on what they have left after taxes. Some people tithe as little as 1% of their income until their faith builds up to 10%. Some people don't tithe at all due to living under the New Covenant as I mentioned but seek out other ways to be generous. **How you do it is between you and God**. That being said.......

I get passionate about tithing. Why? Many reasons. Primarily, tithing is a foundational act of worship and can set us free from what is called "the love of money" (1 Timothy 6:10). To me, this act of worship regarding tithing is not based on the law but on a heart that wants to turn back to Him what He's given to me.

When it comes to tithing, freedom is at stake for the follower of Christ. Set yourself free from your attachment to money and all it can offer you and trust the Lord with your finances. God will honor that and you will have a practical opportunity to see how the Lord will provide for you time and time again just as I have.

* "A poverty mentality says I can't tithe. A rebellious mentality says I won't tithe. A kingdom mentality says how can I not tithe? He's been so good to me. How can I give more?" - Dustin M. Bates

Jen's Coaching Questions:

1. What are your thoughts on tithing?

2. If you've tested God in this way, how has it worked out for you?

3. What do you think about the quote above by Dustin M. Bates?

4. Why do you think the bible usually says to not test God, but in this ONE case, encourages us to - how does that link to New Covenant living?

HOW TO CHOOSE A CHURCH (JEN)

Introductory Thoughts: So, God has recently opened your heart and you've entered into a relationship with Him. You may or may not have heard from other Christ followers that going to church is a good idea. You decide you might like to try it but don't know where to start.

Read:

- 1 Corinthians 4 & 12
- not giving up meeting together, as some are in the habit of doing, but encouraging one another—and all the more as you see the Day approaching. (Hebrews 10:25)
- 20 Above all, you must understand that no prophecy of Scripture came about by the prophet's own interpretation of things. 21 For prophecy never had its origin in the human will, but prophets, though human, spoke from God

as they were carried along by the Holy Spirit. (2 Peter 1:20-21)

- [16] All Scripture is God-breathed and is useful for teaching, rebuking, correcting and training in righteousness, [17] so that the servant of God[a] may be thoroughly equipped for every good work. (2 Timothy 3:16-17)

Now the Berean Jews were of more noble character than those in Thessalonica, for they received the message with great eagerness and examined the Scriptures every day to see if what Paul said was true. (Acts 17:11)

It's true. When you're walking with Christ, it's important to join a church body. In the bible we see Paul tell the Corinthians (and us) the church is a body of believers, that we as Christ followers are the church. Then the author of Hebrews also declares that in being such, we must encourage and equip each other by regularly meeting as the church (Hebrews 10:25). In this chapter, we are going to look at how to choose a church by looking at four unique and biblical components.

Although, this list of how to choose a church is certainly not the way by any means (I'm not that self-righteous or legalistic – haha, this is simply what I would look for in a church if I were on the hunt. So, if you trust me, let's go on the hunt for a group of believers that: teaches Jesus, is outward focused, develops and equips disciples, and feels like family!

A Church that Bases All Teachings off What we Know of Jesus

This is important. Of course, you can probably only find this out after attending a few weeks. So, obviously, it's a process.

How do you know if they teach Jesus?

- Check out their website and see if they state their core beliefs. You're looking for statements along the lines of "the bible is the ONLY authority" or the "complete and inerrant source". Basically, you want to know that they teach the bible and nothing but the bible. If they state any other books that they hold up to the Bible as equal in value, that's a red flag.
- Check out any podcasts or vodcasts on their website and listen to them. Does everything they say glorify God or do they rarely ever mention Him or Jesus? Do they share more of their

opinion, teachings from the world, or truth from the Bible?

- Whether you hear a sermon live or online, match up everything they're saying to the Bible yourself. Why? Because preachers are human. An occasional mistake in their "relaying of the message" is probably just innocent and you can kindly and humbly point it out in an email to them. If you can't be humble and kind, leave it be. If, however, they're making mistakes regularly.... red flag!
- *side note: even if you've been going to a good bible believing church for years, you should ALWAYS study the scriptures yourself after you hear a message.

A Church that is Outward Focused

At our church, we have something we call the Code. I believe we may have ripped a big part of it from Craig Groeschel haha. Anyway, one of my favorite parts states, "the church does not exist for us; we are the church and we exist for the world." If a church is inwardly focused (only caring about the needs of its current members), how are they accomplishing the Great Commission which says to **go** and make disciples of all nations, baptizing them in the name of the Father and of the Son and of the Holy Spirit, [20] and teaching them to obey everything I have commanded? (Matthew 28:16-20)?! The Great Commission commands all Christ followers to go ***out*** into their spheres of influence and even beyond that to make more Christ followers. I once heard someone say "if your church closed its doors tomorrow, would your community even notice?" If you can honestly answer no about a place, then that's not a good sign, friends!*

You'll know if your church is outward focused through their service in the community, how they're giving to the community, and by examining the purpose behind their events. If everything seems to be just for the people inside the church, then it is not outward focused.

A Church that Develops and Equips Disciples

What's the point of church if we're not helping each other grow? Every single one of us has gifts that need to be used. Every single one of us needs to be learning more about God and growing closer to Him daily. Find out if the church you're considering is doing this and find out how. Many churches use small groups to disciple people. Every church should have a place where you can serve/volunteer that will utilize and develop the unique way God has wired you. If the church you're considering doesn't, offer to help them develop it or reconsider your involvement there.

Making disciples who make disciples who make disciples is why we're here on earth. It was the driving force behind the apostle's such as Peter, Paul and the others' ministry and it should be with ours too. God did not mean for us to come to believe in Him and then just sit. We should be growing, investing in others to help them grow, and continuing on with that cycle. If it's not a focus of the church, they're not living out the mission the way God designed.

A Church that Feels Like Family

One thing my church is known for is making every single person who walks in the door feel like family; to feel like they belong. This is vital because if the church is people and not just a place to meet, then where you gather should feel like a safe haven because you're all there...welcoming each other, excited to see each other, offering a safe refuge from the harsh world and a shoulder to lean on. It really is true that "there's no place like home". Don't let the church you're a part of be the exception.

If you walk into a certain church building and don't get greeted for weeks or the same people keep asking your name over and over and over again every time you come, or they keep re-introducing themselves every time they see you even if they did happen to forget your name (I mean it happens) they honestly don't even recognize your face!... that doesn't sound like home to me.

There are many verses that touch on being in the "family of God". Here are a few for example:

- Therefore, as we have opportunity, let us do good to all people, especially to those who belong to the family of believers. (Galatians 6:10)
- If one part suffers, every part suffers with it; if one part is honored, every part rejoices with it. (1 Corinthians 12:26)
- so in Christ we, though many, form one body, and each member belongs to all the others. (Romans 12:5)
- Consequently, you are no longer foreigners and strangers, but fellow citizens with God's people

and also members of his household, (Ephesians 2:19)

- [1] See what great love the Father has lavished on us, that we should be called children of God! And that is what we are! The reason the world does not know us is that it did not know him. [2] Dear friends, now we are children of God, and what we will be has not yet been made known. But we know that when Christ appears,[a] we shall be like him, for we shall see him as he is. (1 John 3:1-2)

Some of the best friendships you will ever have can be formed inside a healthy church. With that said, on to the next chapter, How to Make Friends in a New Church!

Jen's Coaching Questions:

1. What would you look for in a church?

2. What would you say is confusing or unneeded in the list of suggestions that's been provided?

HOW TO MAKE FRIENDS IN A NEW CHURCH (JEN)

Introductory Thoughts: Going to church can be scary. You may feel isolated and alone. You're even new to this whole Jesus thing. Will you fit in? Will you be accepted? How are you to make friends in a place like this?

Read:

- Each of you should use whatever gift you have received to serve others, as faithful stewards of God's grace in its various forms. (1 Peter 4:10)
- [13] you, my brothers and sisters, were called to be free. But do not use your freedom to indulge the flesh[a]; rather, serve one another humbly in love. [14] For the entire law is fulfilled in keeping this one command: "Love your neighbor as yourself."[b] (Galatians 5:13-14)
- [1] Therefore if you have any encouragement from being united with Christ, if any comfort from

his love, if any common sharing in the Spirit, if
any tenderness and compassion, 2 then make my
joy complete by being like-minded, having the
same love, being one in spirit and of one mind.
3 Do nothing out of selfish ambition or vain
conceit. Rather, in humility value others above
yourselves, 4 not looking to your own interests
but each of you to the interests of the others. 5
In your relationships with one another, have the
same mindset as Christ Jesus: 6 Who, being in
very nature[a] God, did not consider equality with
God something to be used to his own advantage;
7 rather, he made himself nothing by taking the
very nature[b] of a servant, being made in human
likeness. 8 And being found in appearance as a
man, he humbled himself by becoming obedient
to death— even death on a cross! 9 Therefore God
exalted him to the highest place and gave him
the name that is above every name, 10 that at the
name of Jesus every knee should bow, in heaven
and on earth and under the earth, 11 and every
tongue acknowledge that Jesus Christ is Lord, to
the glory of God the Father. (Philippians 2:1-11)

- A generous person will prosper; whoever refreshes others will be refreshed. (Proverbs 11:25)

- Carry each other's burdens, and in this way you will fulfill the law of Christ. (Galatians 6:2)
- Share with the Lord's people who are in need. Practice hospitality. (Romans 12:13)

There are three solid ways to make friends at church: find a place to serve, join a small group, and hang out in the lobby! Now, let's take a look at how and why these things work.

Find a Place to Serve

Serving is always a good way to make friends. Why? Because when you work elbow to elbow alongside somebody sharing a common goal, how can a relationship NOT form? When you're working alongside somebody, you tend to share details of your life, find commonality, and develop a deep respect for the other person as you become acquainted with their heart and witness their invaluable work ethic first hand.

Not only that, but by default you'll probably have common interests with those you serve alongside because you already know you share one common interest: serving! If you're serving in the kitchen, you both obviously love to cook, or if you're serving on a worship team together, you both obviously love music! See what I'm saying? Serving is a no brainer way to find friends with whom you share common interests!

Join a Small Group

Joining a small group is another fantastic way to form relationships that will last a lifetime! When you join a small group, you make it a priority to spend intentional time two to four times a month with other people, learning more about each other and God!

At my church, we call them LifeGroups. Our LifeGroups are groups of 8 to 12 people that gather in someone's home once a week for 8 weeks at a time with one month breaks in between sessions. The purpose is to grow closer to God and "do life together". Our LifeGroups are sermon based so we use the time to dive deeper into whatever the topic of the most current Sunday sermon is. In doing that, we learn a lot about each other and the God we serve. Christians that are further along on their journey with Jesus help those just starting out by sharing experiences and answering questions, and those that are just starting their journey with the Lord remind us "old timers" what a joy and what excitement it is to get to know Jesus.

We also use our LifeGroups to meet our needs in practical and tangible ways. When someone in our church has a need, we direct them to their LifeGroup (if they're in one) before we direct them to the church staff. Whether it's a financial need, a hospital visit, helping someone move, setting up a meal train or simply saying a prayer, your LifeGroup is there to serve you and in turn, experience you serving them as well. It's a beautiful thing and so meaningful!

LifeGroups truly become family! There's something so amazing about knowing you have a group of people you can go to no matter what, people who have your back and know you have theirs! If your church offers small groups, inquire about them today!

Hang Out in the Lobby

I don't know why but this one makes me giggle. It seems so simple and obvious, I guess, yet so many of us walk straight from the parking lot into the gathering and then dart right back out as soon as the closing prayer is said. May I discourage you from that?! Show up 15 minutes early and mingle in the lobby or in the cafe (if your church has one). Find someone you don't recognize and walk up to them and ask "Forgive me if we already have, but have we met yet? I'm so and so..." If you have met, say "oh! That's right! So what do you think about this current sermon series?" I mean honestly, ask whatever you want. Say whatever you want. Just open your mouth! This is important for many reasons:

- You should not expect your pastoral staff to do all the "meeting of people" in the lobby. This is YOUR church too! Act like it and take ownership!
- Constituents or guests will begin to believe that everyone who attends there cares about them; not just the staff.
- Your confidence will grow. Believe me; I always feel stupid striking up a conversation with someone I may or may not already know (who can remember in a church of several hundred?) I always feel stupid if I have met them before like I'm some kind of snob but I simply laugh, apologize and move on in the conversation. Being REAL is better than being distant.
- The more you meet people over time, the more you'll feel at home when you're inside your church building! It's like Cheers! <u>You wanna go where everybody knows your name! "Hey, Norm!"</u>

So there you have it. I hope the idea of making friends at a new church seems a little less daunting for you. If you're brand spanking new, find a place to serve and join a small group. If you've been there for a month or two, hang out in the lobby before or after church. You'll soon be more popular than you'd ever realized...or maybe even wanted to be. Ha!

*Additionally, I want to suggest that all the above suggestions are adaptable for online attendance as well! Ask your online campus pastor about serving opportunities such as Small Groups. As for hanging out in the lobby, be sure to comment on church posts and reply to the comments of others! Then, also send friend requests or follow any new people you meet at the online gathering on Sundays!

Jen's Coaching Questions:

1. Name one person you've met online or in person at church recently. How can you get to know them?

2. What are some things you wish people at church would do to get to know you? How can you take initiative in that?

WHY SHOULD I GO TO CHURCH? (JEN)

Introductory Thoughts: Okay, so you tried church but you're just not digging it. Let's explore that for a minute.

Read:

- Every day they continued to meet together in the temple courts. They broke bread in their homes and ate together with glad and sincere hearts, (Acts 2:46)
- 1 Corinthians 12-14,
- not giving up meeting together, as some are in the habit of doing, but encouraging one another—and all the more as you see the Day approaching. (Hebrews 10:25)

Why should I go to church? It's a valid question. I mean our excuses...er...reasons seem valid!

- I believe in God. I can worship Him anywhere.

- I'm busy and can't sacrifice an hour on Sunday.
- I can listen to the message online!

Growing up, it was my family's culture to attend church every Sunday and often Wednesday too! We went for the community, we went to show our love and devotion to God, and we went because it was important to show in a tangible way what we valued as a family, together as a family. However, culture changes doesn't it?

Christian families have by and large gone from attending church twice a week with the rare exception, to attending once a month. Once a month is the new norm due to sports activities, working on the weekends and dare I say ....families not understanding the relevance of physical attendance anymore.

With that in mind, I'd like to invite you into a little perspective shift and help you understand why you should go to church as often as possible. The five reasons you simply can't ignore are because of community, corporate worship, using your gifts, hearing the word, and my favorite...because God said so.

#1. Go to Church to Enjoy Community

People, we go for community. There's something about walking into a building or a room where everyone there (or most everyone there) knows they're innately flawed, but holds on to hope and seeks to share the love of Jesus. We go to check in on each other (how are you? Did you get that job? Is your kid feeling better?) Yes, you can do that on FaceBook but it means so much more when they see the care in your eyes and feel the warmth of your hug. There's something about your kids seeing their friends and you seeing your friends all together in the same place because Jesus is that important! I don't know about you but I want my family to be able to walk into at least one place weekly, where most everyone are excited to see them, where they experience being valued, and loved.

If we value spending time with our blood family via nightly dinners around the table, vacations, bedtime routines and more, shouldn't we value regularly and intentionally meeting up with our Jesus family too? Make it a priority to see your church family face to face. In fact, go even further than a Sunday gathering, and join a small group (Acts 2:46) if your church offers them. We were made for community and it'll help us grow spiritually when we're walking through life together.

Now, I know life gets crazy and sometimes you can't go to church in person. In these cases, church online or on social media is totally okay! Be sure to make the most of it while you're there though - comment during the worship and sermon parts of the gathering, respond to other people's comments, respond to prayer requests and react (like, heart, care emoji) to the comments of others. You can even take it a step further and send friend requests to others attending! Where have I heard that before?

#2. Go to Church to Worship with Others

We go to worship alongside others. Yes, you can worship to Hillsong by yourself in your car, but boy oh boy is it a great experience to hear the person on your left singing completely out of tune with deep love to our savior, and to hear the other on your right sing like an angel and you think, "man, this must be just a touch of what heaven is like". There is NO experience like it. Worshiping in a room full of worshipers is a life-giving, energizing, hope filling experience where The Holy Spirit loves to do some of His best work! Don't cheat yourself out of that experience and opportunity! And give God the glory He deserves!

#3. Go to Church to Use Your Gifts

God has blessed each one of us with natural talents and spiritual gifts that we are told to use to serve others (1 Peter 4). Yes, you can and should use them outside of the church but you must use them inside the church too. The church is described as a body with many parts, each with their own function (1 Corinthians 12-14) and you're part of that. Your church wouldn't be the same if you weren't there using your gifts. If you don't know what your spiritual gifts are, you should take a spiritual gifts inventory or ask your pastor about one.

#4. Go to Church to Hear the Word

We go to hear the Word. I know, I know...we can listen to the podcast or watch the vodcast online BUT once again I say, it's sooo much better in person! There's a feeling in the room when a truth hits home. There's an opportunity to squeeze your friend's hand when a chord is struck. There's a chance to tell your pastor in person you appreciated his or her obedience in sharing God's word. Additionally, unlike the distractions at home that can pull you away from staying focused on the podcast, when you're sitting in an auditorium and your kids are elsewhere receiving God's word, you can take detailed notes to study later and go deeper into the Word.

And (wink wink, nudge nudge) let's be honest, when life is this busy, we often find it hard to make time for church online too. Therefore, you might as well make the effort to go.

5. Go to Church Because God Said So

And last, but certainly not least, we need to go to church because God said so. Hebrews 10:25 says we ought not to be "neglecting to meet together, as is the habit of some, but encouraging one another, and all the more as you see the Day drawing near" (ESV).

We should not give up meeting together. We must stay together. We need each other to encourage one another. We need the accountability. And we as the body are called to point each other in a loving way away from sin and back to Jesus. These things are so much harder to do unless you're regularly and physically meeting together. And because it's a command from God, we should be treating it so.

One More Reason

And you know what? I'm gonna throw one more reason in...go to church in order to love, encourage, and support your pastor(s). Your pastor(s) and staff live and breathe serving the local church. Every day they're praying for you, visiting you, supporting you, planning for you, learning for you and so much more. And their favorite day of the week? Sunday. On Sunday, they wake up not only excited to go and see the fruits of their labor, but go see the faces of all those that God loves and has called them to serve. On Sundays they see their WHOLE church family gathered in one place for a common purpose. It's a thing of true beauty that makes all the work and effort worth it and gives them a glimpse of what heaven will be like someday. When you're not there, they notice it; they feel it, and they miss you.

Okay, okay. So, all that being said, life still happens. I get it. All I'm trying to convey is that face to face meeting with your brothers and sisters in Christ is so important that you need to make it a priority as often as you can. I hope I've impressed that upon you in this piece of writing. What are your plans to make going to church a priority? Or do you still not see the validity in regular attendance?

<u>Jen's Coaching Questions:</u>

1. Why would you say church is necessary?
2. Why would you say church is unnecessary?
3. Going to church is just meeting with the church since the church is a body of believers and not a building. Even when you can't make it to church for whatever reason, how can you BE the church in your everyday life?

BIBLE GHOST STORIES: WHO IS THE HOLY SPIRIT? (JEN)

Introductory Thoughts: This is very rudimentary and may catch you off guard but as a Christ follower, it's important that you know about the trinity. The trinity is a concept of a Godhead who is three persons in one; God, Jesus, and the Holy Spirit. A version of this piece was originally written and published elsewhere with an audience aged 6-12 in mind or for those who teach them. I hope it accurately introduces you to the person and concept of The Holy Spirit as well.

Read:

- For to us a child is born, to us a son is given, and the government will be on his shoulders. And he will be called Wonderful Counselor, Mighty God, Everlasting Father, Prince of Peace. (Isaiah 9:6)

- Peter replied, "Repent and be baptized, every one of you, in the name of Jesus Christ for the forgiveness of your sins. And you will receive the gift of the Holy Spirit. (Acts 2:38)
- 16 And I will ask the Father, and he will give you another advocate to help you and be with you forever— 17 the Spirit of truth. The world cannot accept him, because it neither sees him nor knows him. But you know him, for he lives with you and will be[a] in you. (John 14:16-17)
- But you will receive power when the Holy Spirit comes on you; and you will be my witnesses in Jerusalem, and in all Judea and Samaria, and to the ends of the earth. (Acts 1:8)

It is often difficult for kids and even adults to understand who the Holy Spirit is and how He helps us.

Let's see if we can navigate through these questions by asking a few others...

Who's ever done something wrong? Or felt bad about it? Who's been brave when most would be scared or was in need of help to make right decisions?

If you said yes to any of the above, you may have had help from Jiminy Cricket (your conscience) or if you said yes AND you've given your life to Jesus, you may have had help from the Holy Spirit!

Who is the Holy Spirit and what does He do? Is He wind? Is He fire? Does He give you superpowers? Maybe you've heard some of these explanations/ comparisons before. Let's find out who He really is once and for all!

Have you ever heard of the TRINITY? God in three persons? What?!?! God in three persons? How is that possible? Well, remember. With God, ALL things are possible! The trinity is God, Jesus, and the Holy Spirit. They are three in one. We know who God is... He MADE us. We know who Jesus is...He SAVED us. But who is the Holy Spirit?

Think of it like this: Think of your Dad or Mom. They are ONE person, but they are a PARENT to you, spouse to each other, friend to their friends, employee to their job, and son or daughter to their parents. They're ALL THESE DIFFERENT PEOPLE but still just ONE PERSON! So, it is basically the same with the trinity.

This helps us understand the trinity but we still need to know who the Holy Spirit is. Let's find out what the bible has to say about him!

1. Who is the Holy Spirit? Isaiah 9:6
2. How do you receive the Holy Spirit? Acts 2:38
3. Where does He live? John 14:16-17
4. What does He do in our lives? Acts 1:8; John 14:26; John 16:8; Galatians 5:22-23

Work as detectives and really answer these questions and discuss them with others if possible.

So, if God MADE us, and Jesus SAVED us, then we can conclude from these verses that the Holy Spirit HELPS US stay in fellowship with Him who saved us and reminds us why and by WHOM we were made! The Holy Spirit HELPS the purposes of Jesus and God which is why they're all three together of ONE MIND and PURPOSE!

The Holy Spirit HELPS the purposes of Jesus and God which is why they're all three together of ONE MIND and PURPOSE!

Jen's Coaching Questions:

1. Who would you say The Holy Spirit is?

2. How would you describe The Holy Spirit?

3. How would you describe the trinity?

4. How does the Holy Spirit help you?

BAPTISM TO STAY AFLOAT (JEN)

Introductory thoughts: So, there's water baptism (which you quickly learned about in Chapter 4) but did you know you can also be baptized in The Holy Spirit? It's true! And now that you know who the Holy Spirit is, it's time to know the Holy Spirit and His power made available to us. This can be hard to grasp, but read on!..

Read:

- Romans 8
- But you will receive power when the Holy Spirit comes on you; and you will be my witnesses in Jerusalem, and in all Judea and Samaria, and to the ends of the earth. (Acts 1:8)
- Acts 2
- Matthew 26:31-75

Because it's hard to grasp, it can also be hard to explain. It's for this reason, that when God gives a perfect depiction through a real life scenario such as my kid's swimming lessons, I get super excited. I do realize that all who may read this book don't believe in Holy Spirit Baptism. If that's you, you have permission to pass this one over; I won't be offended...but I hope you won't. ;)

"Ugh! I've done it again! I'm such a failure! I am too weak and therefore will never be effective for God or any call He places on my life....." If we're all honest, we've all proclaimed something similar to ourselves whether audibly or thoughtfully in a moment of unintentional or unexpected sin. We love the Lord. We've confessed our sins and asked Him into our hearts and we take up our cross daily.... only to stumble and drop it too many times to count, and more than enough times to make us feel like powerless failures.

We know that Paul himself admitted that he finds himself doing the things he doesn't want to do and not doing the things he wants to or knows he should do (Romans 7:15, NIV). Often in despair and anguish over failing again in our own human strength and letting Jesus down, we find ourselves singing the lyrics of a popular christian song, "Do you still feel the nails every time I fail? Can you hear the crowd cry crucify again?....." We are devastated that in our human weakness, we have fallen into temptation again and we wonder, "how is it even possible to have the power or the strength to stand firm for Jesus?"

How is it even possible to have the power or the strength to stand firm for Jesus?

Let me tell you about a guy named Peter. He was passionately dedicated to Jesus - to the point of cutting off an ear of one he viewed as an enemy to Jesus. He believed himself ready to do anything that Jesus would need him to do as his friend and follower. He was shocked when Jesus told him that very soon he'd actually deny even knowing him three times! Peter was aghast! - No way would that ever happen! He was sure of it.

But... then Jesus got taken away by some government officials. Peter stayed close at hand to see what would happen to him and while waiting and watching, three people recognized him as a follower and friend of Jesus, calling him out as so. Guess what? Peter denied all three accusations out of fear. (Matthew 26:31-75)

Oh Peter. Imagine the devastation and heartbreak he experienced when he heard the rooster crow (Luke

22:54-62, NIV). He had a powerful love and dedication to Jesus and thought himself firm and strong enough that it seemed incredulous to him that he could ever possibly deny Jesus and let him down in that way. However, the truth emerged and Peter realized that no matter how much you love Jesus and no matter how strong you are, you are still weak in your own power.

God knows this about us and that is why He provided an answer to our frailty. God knows we fail, but if our hearts are truly repentant, He has prepared a gift especially for us...to help us in our weakness. This gift is the baptism in the Holy Spirit. He is part of the God Head three in one (Mark 1:9-11, NIV) and gives us power to do the things God asks of us (Romans 8:26 and Acts 1:8, NIV).

We see evidence of the benefits of receiving the baptism in the Holy Spirit as our counselor, again in the book of Peter. On the day of Pentecost, (Acts 2, NIV) just weeks after Peter so miserably failed Jesus by denying him because he feared the reactions of the people, we find him BOLDLY addressing the curiosity of the crowds about the happenings of Pentecost by preaching his first sermon recorded in the book of Acts, subsequently causing 3000 people to be saved ! The same man who was cowardly only weeks before has now made a powerful friend in the Holy Spirit who gives him boldness and strength to do the things he ought to do. The Holy Spirit is available here and now to do that for you too. In that Pentecost sermon, Peter declared that " ...the promise is for you and your children and all who are far off...."(Acts 2:38-39, NIV)

Our problem in being able to receive the baptism in the Holy Spirit often lies in another human weakness...... the complexity of our minds and our inability to rationalize the simplicity of receiving this free and generous gift. It's like with my son, Aiden, when he was 5. He took swimming lessons and couldn't seem to conquer the almighty back float. I explained to him that when swimmers are tired or weak, the ability to float is a gift God has the water provide for us to help us out. All he has to do is relax, tilt his chin up towards heaven, and open his arms wide as if wanting a big hug from Jesus.....and then, without even realizing it or really trying, the water will mysteriously and mystically ENABLE him and lift him up and support him! Although he heard this, his five year old mind couldn't logically comprehend and trust that it's so. He therefore would get scared and try to do the work on his own by twisting his body and kicking his legs which only caused him to fail and sink every time.

If we want baptism in the Holy Spirit, all we have to do is ask and receive (Matthew 7:7-11, Acts 2:38, NIV). We don't have to force anything. It's a free gift...the same as salvation (Romans 6:23, NIV). It requires no work on our part but to ask and take what God has so graciously offered us through Jesus Christ. When the baptism is underway, the Holy Spirit will ENABLE you by giving you His manifest presence and impressions of what to pray. All we need to do is relax, receive and have faith to obey.

There are, however, things that can hinder us from the gift of baptism in the Holy Spirit just as there are things that can hinder Aiden from floating. The bible shows us that obedience, unity and time with Jesus are important in receiving this baptism (Acts 1-2, NIV). So, if you lack these, you may be hindered. Just as Aiden needs to obey and relax as he's instructed, trusting how the water works, with how he was made, and spending time practicing to float. If Aiden lacks one of these aspects, he will be hindered from his goal of floating.

It's simple to receive the gift Jesus has for us...go to him in prayer, ask and then, simply wait to receive. If you find you're waiting longer than expected, check that there's nothing hindering you from "staying afloat". But, if you're relaxed and simply tilt your chin up, and open your arms wide toward heaven to receive, you'll soon find yourself unexpectedly filled and supported by a mystical and mysterious power! Aiden's manifestation of success will be evidenced in the mysterious ability to stay afloat. Your manifestation will come with mysterious groans that words cannot express (Romans 8:26, NIV).

Jen's Coaching Questions:

1. If you're baptized in the Holy Spirit, reflect on how you received that gift. How would you explain it to someone who is yet to receive it?

2. If you're not yet baptized in the Holy Spirit, what do you think the hold up may be?

3. How come no matter how much we love Jesus and no matter how strong we are, we are still weak?

4. How do you think Peter felt when he gave his first sermon on Pentecost?

5. Do you think nearly as many people would have been saved that day if Peter wasn't filled with the Holy Spirit? Why or why not?

USING MY GIFTS (MEGAN)

Introductory Thoughts: You've been created by God on purpose, for a purpose. Even before the foundation of the world, before you ever existed, God wrote a story about your life. As He says in Psalm 139:16 "You saw me before I was born. Every day of my life was recorded in your book. Every moment was laid out before a single day had passed."

God made no mistakes when He fashioned your being and defined who you are. We've covered your identity in Christ. You are God's beloved, precious child who He chose to be His own. And now that you're in Christ, part of the adventure of following Him is discovering the unique person you are and the spiritual gifts He placed inside of you.

Read:

- 1 Corinthians 12
- 13 For you created my inmost being; you knit me together in my mother's womb. 14 I praise you

because I am fearfully and wonderfully made; your works are wonderful, I know that full well. [15] My frame was not hidden from you when I was made in the secret place, when I was woven together in the depths of the earth. [16] Your eyes saw my unformed body; all the days ordained for me were written in your book before one of them came to be. (Psalm 139:13-16)

- [6] For this reason I remind you to fan into flame the gift of God, which is in you through the laying on of my hands. [7] For the Spirit God gave us does not make us timid, but gives us power, love and self-discipline. (2 Timothy 1:6-7)
- Matthew 25:14-30

What are spiritual gifts?

Spiritual gifts are God-given abilities or talents that are different for everyone. They are part of who you are and can't be added to or ever taken away from you (Romans 11:29). They're part of God's design for your life and will help you fulfill what He has called you to do. Your gifts were placed inside of you by God when He planned for you to come into the world. They go deep because they are part of who you are. They are referred to as "gifts" because they can't be earned or bought; they are simply what God chose to place in you so that one day you could use them for His glory and to show others who He is.

Examples of spiritual gifts include administration, apostleship, discernment, evangelism, exhortation, faith, giving, healing, helps, hospitality, knowledge, leadership, mercy, prophecy, serving, speaking in tongues, teaching, and wisdom.

People who follow Jesus are collectively referred to as the Body of Christ (1 Corinthians 12), a beautiful concept that means we are all connected, all part of God's family, and all have important functions that both fulfill and satisfy us and compliment others. Learning about your gifts helps you function at your best as a useful part of the body. Notably, in addition to functioning at your best capacity, you'll also be aiding other parts of the body to be at their best.

Learning about your gifts helps you function at your best as a useful part of the body.

To illustrate how the body works together, let's say you break your leg and have to walk on crutches for a period of time. Because your leg is broken, your whole body will have to adjust and compensate for the broken leg. You'll walk differently, your routines will change and more of your attention will be spent on dealing with the leg. The rest of your body has to adjust and change based on what's happening with the leg. Once your leg is healed up, healthy and functioning as it should, it helps your whole body be in balance and it can provide the support it was made for.

How do you discover and use your spiritual gifts?

Using your gifts helps you lead a fulfilling life as a Christian, because you'll be able to live with great purpose and also experience the satisfaction that comes from doing what you're made for.

There are a few key ways you can learn about your gifts:

-Speak with friends, mentors and pastors about characteristics they've noticed in you

-Take a spiritual gifts test: a good online resource to begin with is giftstest.com.

-Begin volunteering in your church! This is hands down the best way to start the process of discovering who you are- by trying different areas of ministry and seeing what works best. It is so exciting to find things you're naturally great at- but there is also no shame in coming to the realization that something is not a good fit for you. In fact it's wise to avoid assumptions or stereotypes because God is very creative and He made you unique! You could begin with any area of volunteering that you're interested in. It won't take long for you to find out if the area is a good fit for you or not. Remember that the goal is for you to be able to do what you are gifted to do, and that will be a huge blessing to everyone around you as you'll be functioning in your specific calling.

Avoiding the Comparison Trap

So, you start discovering your gifts and begin to get excited about what you can do. You begin to step out in faith trusting God to teach you and guide you as you learn to function within your calling. But then, you start looking at people around you who seem more gifted or have callings which place them in positions to be looked up to- or you see others who have different gifts and decide yours are better. It's easy to compare yourself to others and either be discouraged or think more highly of yourself than you ought.

Once comparisons enter the conversation, nobody wins except the enemy of your soul. Teddy Roosevelt said it this way: "Comparison is the thief of joy." We encourage you to guard against the trap of comparison by doing the following:

- Get excited about your own unique contributions to the kingdom of God. There are things you can do that nobody else can do quite like you. Regardless of what you're called to do, we as the Body need you and we all need each other. You've been placed in your church and in your life situations by God's design and He is ready to help you grow in fulfilling your calling.

Once comparison enters the conversation, nobody wins except the enemy of your soul.

- Maintain an attitude of humility and serve others as modeled by Jesus (Philippians 2:1-11)

- Celebrate and rejoice when others are used by God

Becoming a great steward of your gifts

In Matthew 25:14-30, Jesus told a story about a man who went on a journey and entrusted different amounts of money to his servants at home. Each was given an amount according to his ability in order that they should use it and see it grow on their master's behalf. When the man returned he asked for an accounting; 2 of the 3 servants had used what was entrusted to them and it multiplied; the master was pleased. But the third guy admitted he did nothing with what he was given. The master was upset with this servant and took his money away and gave it to the ones who had used theirs.

Now the point of this story is not that Jesus is waiting to be upset with anyone. The point is that you have been called and given purpose by God and that using it is a matter of responsibility. The cool thing is that because it belongs to God, it is from Him and already possesses the potential to grow and bless the master. YOU possess the potential to grow and bless Jesus in using what He gave you.

Note that everyone is given different amounts according to ability. God in His wisdom knows how much to give you and He only asks that you trust Him and step forward in faith to use it. He doesn't ask you to use someone else's gifts, to look like anyone else, or to be responsible for others. Each is responsible for his or her own gift use.

Why does using gifts require courage and trust? Because you are actively moving forward to do something. Even if you don't get it right. Even when you make mistakes. Instead of waiting for things to happen to you, using your gifts is learning to be an active disciple of Jesus and trusting He will be there to use what you offer and help you.

Remember, these are God's talents and He is the one who will make them grow. Knowing that Jesus has got your back and that He desires you to use your gifts helps you to be brave in taking steps to do so. The outcome is then God's to handle; your part is to move ahead and use what He gave you.

Another key concept in this story is the reason that Servant #3 gave for letting his talents remain idle: Fear. Plain old ugly, paralyzing fear. Whenever you step out into doing something for God, you will face fear. But courage is not the absence of fear; it's acting in spite of the fear and "doing it afraid."

God has given you victory in Christ- sometimes walking out this victory means we are facing down fear in unlikely places. It means Jesus is there to teach you to overcome and go deeper in your relationship with Him as you do so.

The unfaithful servant said "I was afraid, so I hid them." He allowed fear to rule him and prevent his potential from being realized. All three guys were given the same assignment. Different talents but the same assignment: *go out and use what I gave you and see what I'll do with it, trusting in Me that there will be fruit and that what you're doing counts.*

God is faithful and Jesus will never leave you. He placed in you a mighty calling and gave you work to do for His kingdom.

You have before you an exciting adventure of finding out how God has gifted you and then using those things to serve Him and others. You might discover a purpose you never knew you had. You might unearth something that deep inside you always knew was there but never got used. There will be some "aha" moments when you find out exactly who God made you to be.

One thing is for certain: operating in your gifts will mean you lead a more fulfilled and joyful life. As you are faithful to step out to discover and use your gifts, God will be there to meet you. The only way you could miss out would be to ignore them, so get to it and start living your purpose.

Megan's Coaching Questions:

1. Are there any spiritual gifts you already know you have?

2. What steps do you need to take to begin volunteering with your church?

3. What does faithfulness in using your gifts look like practically in your everyday life?

WALKING IN FREEDOM: GRACE AND THE R-WORD (MEGAN)

Introductory Thoughts: Here's what you need to know about grace: It changes absolutely everything. The grace of God could keep us endlessly talking and writing, it is so great and so amazing.

God's grace is over your life as a follower of Jesus. Grace makes the difference between trying to live your life in your own strength and all on your own and being helped and led by the Spirit of God. Grace says to you: even when you make mistakes, fail, and utterly lose track, I, the Lord, am here to catch you, heal you, tell you it's okay.

Along with grace comes the importance of repentance (turning away from sin) as we keep growing and as God purifies and renews our lives for Christ. In this chapter we'll talk about how both grace and repentance are key to living for Jesus.

Read:

- Romans 6
- Romans 8
- Do not conform to the pattern of this world, but be transformed by the renewing of your mind. Then you will be able to test and approve what God's will is—his good, pleasing and perfect will. (Romans 12:2)
- And we all, who with unveiled faces contemplate[a] the Lord's glory, are being transformed into his image with ever-increasing glory, which comes from the Lord, who is the Spirit. (2 Corinthians 3:18)
- [22] You were taught, with regard to your former way of life, to put off your old self, which is being corrupted by its deceitful desires; [23] to be made new in the attitude of your minds; [24] and to put on the new self, created to be like God in true righteousness and holiness. (Ephesians 4:22-24)
- [1] Follow God's example, therefore, as dearly loved children [2] and walk in the way of love, just as Christ loved us and gave himself up for

us as a fragrant offering and sacrifice to God. (Ephesians 5:1-2)

- To this you were called, because Christ suffered for you, leaving you an example, that you should follow in his steps.(1 Peter 2:21)

- Grace is the difference between a life lived in bondage or a life full of freedom.

Grace means you live under God's love, understanding and acceptance, regardless of your own shortcomings and all the things that grieve and beset you.

You do not need to earn your salvation because Jesus has already done that. Becoming His follower doesn't mean that you're out if you don't follow all the rules; it means you are seeking Jesus and accepting Him as Lord and Savior; He will lead you and become your teacher. Jesus has freed you from having to be perfect in order to earn His approval. You now live a life washed by His blood, and He gives you power through the Holy Spirit to live for Him.

Romans 6:11 tells us to "count yourselves dead to sin but alive to God in Christ Jesus" and verse 14 says "For sin shall no longer be your master, because you are not under the law, but under grace."

The "law" is a reference to the old covenant, which existed before Jesus and required that people follow a long list of rules and do certain things to be right with God. That concept of earning God's approval is not unlike other religions with their requirements.

Jesus came to earth in human flesh, died on the cross for our sins and came back to life, thereby offering salvation by grace through faith, changing everything. He fulfilled all of the old requirements and set us free from them. The old laws help us understand right from wrong and help us define what sin is but they do not have any power over us.

Instead of making behavioral requirements the central focus of your repentance, Jesus invites you to have a relationship with Him in which knowing Him changes you starting from the condition of your heart which then positively affects your behaviors. This doesn't mean you won't have struggles and need forgiveness on a daily basis.

You're now God's child, and your identity is secure in Him, but you will still need God's forgiveness when you fall short. Only Jesus has ever walked this earth without sin.

God's grace is free and without requirement. Jesus is the one who paid for sin and it doesn't need to be paid for again, not now or in the future. Grace means God's unconditional love is just that- no strings attached.

> God's grace is free and without requirement.

It's important to remember that there will be times in your journey when you fail, fall short and miss the mark. Times when you can't believe that God would forgive you and times you become discouraged in your walk with Jesus. When this happens, train yourself to run to Jesus, not away from him. He won't be surprised by your actions since he already knows what's up. The enemy of your soul would have you hide from God and push yourself further into whatever is holding you back; but don't fall for it. Instead, as soon as you realize you need God's forgiveness, don't hesitate. Run to Him, repent and ask for His forgiveness. His grace means He is waiting to forgive and restore you, not punish or condemn you.

> train yourself to run to Jesus, not away from him.

When you make a mistake or are dealing with a sin issue, remember that Jesus is ready to forgive you.

When you need help you can come freely before the throne of grace and find mercy and grace from God. (Hebrews 4:16)

The truth is in the understanding that we live under grace because of Jesus and that as one of His disciples we are being transformed by knowing Him. The more we know Jesus, the more we change; even the things that we desire change as God works in our hearts over time. He changes us through His word, through other people in our lives, through situations that cause us to seek Him in deeper ways, through experiencing His presence when we worship and spend time with Him.

God is always at work fashioning and shaping us. This is because of His grace. Even the fact that you desire to grow and be more like Jesus and are reading this book is evidence of God's beautiful grace at work within you.

Grace is also defined as "unmerited favor." It is freely given by God as the inclination or ability to do what we can't do on our own. We did not and cannot earn it.

Grace is the help from God to do what you can't do in your own ability or strength, and the permission to be imperfect and need help and forgiveness from Jesus and others as you grow.

The R-Word- Repentance

But what about life change? Is being a disciple of Jesus only about being forgiven and free and doing whatever you want? Nope. Jesus Himself spoke about the high cost of discipleship when he spoke about following Him (Matthew 16:24-27). Living for Jesus means you are free from the power of sin, and you now make the choice to live out your salvation (Philippians 2:12-13) on a daily basis.

We live under grace, but as we follow Jesus, He will root out and remove sins, hindrances and old patterns as we are transformed and becoming more like Him.

The key to being rid of sin and growing more like Christ: our repentance.

Jesus calls you to deny yourself and to become like Him. This means some things are going to change.

"Repentance" can be an intimidating word- most people think it involves punishment or the wrath of God. Really, the Biblical word "repentance" simply means to turn 180 degrees and go in the other direction. It really is the letting go of things which keep you from God and making a total turnaround in your life with God's help.

Repentance is an act of your will. It's about true brokenness and commitment to change, not saying you're sorry so you can be cleansed only to go out and sin again. It's what you do when you're ready to turn away from sin and experience the power of Jesus to help you change. It is coming before God with honesty and keeping nothing from Him. Even if God already knows what you've done, your honesty and earnestness matters to Him because that's how He changes your heart and heals you from your sin.

Sin will always keep you from the abundant life of Christ. As the saying goes, sin will always cost you (and others) more than you wanted to pay and always keep you longer than you wanted to stay.

Repentance is important and is a gift to us, because it breaks the power of sin in your heart.

Hebrews 12:1 says "Therefore, since we are surrounded by such a great cloud of witnesses (those who have gone before us in the faith whose stories are told in Scripture), let us throw off everything that hinders and the sin that so easily entangles. And let us run with perseverance the race marked out for us."

You've got a race to run for Christ and to run well you need to be free and unburdened. People mistakenly think that if they follow Christ they'll be weighed down by requirements; when in truth you'll be set free from sin and its entanglements and travel lighter than ever.

Jesus taught that we should be ruthless in dealing with sin, digging it out and giving it no place (Matthew 5:29-30). Why should we be ruthless with it when we are also under grace?

Graphic story alert: In ancient Rome there was a punishment that involved strapping a maggot-infested rotting corpse to the back of a criminal. As the person carried this dead body on his back, it weighed him down and slowly leaked poisons into his body. The result of course was an unimaginable slow death involving crushing weight, sickness, and horrific pain.

This is what happens to our souls when sin stuff isn't dealt with. Sin harms us, weighs us down, keeps us from what is life-giving and is ultimately deadly (spiritually and even sometimes relationally and/or physically).

You were not designed to live out your days crushed under the weight of lesser things. You were designed to love God, be in a life-giving relationship with Him, adore Him and be helpful to others as God uses you for His purposes.

Without repentance, the darkness which holds you back will keep being a hindrance and tripping you up- robbing you of all that God has for you. God has so much more for you. Jesus loves you and wants you to be truly free. He wants you to be unburdened and able to serve Him, living in abundant joy as you walk out your faith.

As you consider repentance, remember that Jesus was sent by God to save us, not condemn us (John 3:17). He is not waiting to punish you but to give you life!

The grace and truth of Jesus

One time when Jesus was getting ready to teach, the Jewish religious leaders brought a woman before him who had been caught in the act of adultery. They, who lived under the law and not grace, wanted to stone her to death for her sin. Jesus, in short order, told them they had just as much stuff going on in their lives and no right to accuse her and sent them away. After he drove away her accusers, he turned to her. To the woman he said "Neither do I condemn you. Go now and leave your life of sin." (John 8:1-12) He simply wanted to free her from sin and offered her the grace to do it.

This is the beauty of growth in Christ: experiencing the grace of God in Jesus and repenting so you can be free to live for Him.

repenting so you can be free to live for Him

Repenting happens in a few different ways. Take some time in prayer to ask God where He wants to set you free. Ask trusted pastors and friends who love you where they might have noticed something that needs to go or isn't quite right. There are times when you already know you need to deal with something.

Other times, God will need to convict you- He will do so but never condemn.

When something needs to go, trust Jesus and repent right away.

When you confess (admit to) sin, you bring it out of the darkness so it is no longer hidden and continues hurting you.You are casting off that nasty corpse that has been strapped to your back.

You can pray and repent on your own before the Lord, and there is also power in confession of sin to others. It's a beautiful thing to share your struggle with someone you can trust who is mature in Christ and can help you through it. James 5:16 says "confess your sins to each other and pray for each other so that you may be healed." Confessing with trusted fellow Christians and pastors is a powerful breaker of bondage.

Psalm 139:23-24 gives us a beautiful picture of a heart after God: "Search me, God, and know my heart; test me and know my anxious thoughts. See if there is any offensive way in me, and lead me in the way everlasting."

We are praying for you as you learn to walk in grace and also let God root out the poisons of sin in your life.

Megan's coaching questions:

1. How would you explain grace to someone who has never heard of it?

2. Why don't we have to follow rules to earn God's approval anymore?

3. Why is repentance important?

Take some time to journal and let God speak to your heart about areas in your life where He wants to help you get free from sin. Then find a fellow believer or pastor to talk with about these areas.

LIVING A LIFE MARKED BY LOVE (JEN)

Introductory Thoughts: I want to make it clear that this book is not meant to be rules and regulations you must follow to hold on to your salvation. There is no formula for following Christ because following Him is based on your relationship with Him and everyone's relationship is different according to the choices they make. This book is meant to be a field guide of best practices to keep your momentum going forward in the most meaningful relationship of your life. And these best practices are coming to you from two gals who've literally been walking this road themselves as well as leading others on it for decades. Now, it's your turn to take the reins for yourself and invite those you meet and know along on the journey. Remember and be encouraged that even the little things make a big difference - do them because you're saved not to be saved or continue to be saved. Megan and I are cheering you on.

Read:

- Dear friends, now we are children of God, and what we will be has not yet been made known. But we know that when Christ appears,[a] we shall be like him, for we shall see him as he is. (I John 3:2)
- 22 But the fruit of the Spirit is love, joy, peace, forbearance, kindness, goodness, faithfulness, 23 gentleness and self-control. Against such things there is no law. (Galatians 5:22-23)
- making the most of every opportunity, because the days are evil. (Ephesians 5:16)
- Be wise in the way you act toward outsiders; make the most of every opportunity. (Colossians 4:5)
- But in your hearts revere Christ as Lord. Always be prepared to give an answer to everyone who asks you to give the reason for the hope that you have. But do this with gentleness and respect, (1 Peter 3:15)
- "I am the vine; you are the branches. If you remain in me and I in you, you will bear much fruit; apart from me you can do nothing. (John 15:5)
- Do not merely listen to the word, and so deceive yourselves. Do what it says. (James 1:22)

Defining Discipleship again

At the beginning of this book we defined discipleship as ***gaining or having the ability to hear from God and obey the Holy Spirit on your own to renew your identity IN Jesus and commitment TO Jesus daily***. Author and Pastor, Carey Nieuwhof, puts it simply that a disciple is "*someone who has decided to* ***trust*** Jesus *as their Savior." But how do you know whether they're following Jesus?*

Jesus actually gave us a very practical test that helps us know. He simply said: "By their fruit you'll recognize them. Do people pick grapes from thorn bushes, or figs from thistles?"

In other words, look at someone's life for the evidence." (Nieuwhof, 5 Unfair Criticisms of Large Churches it's Time to Drop)

If you want to know if you're hearing from God and committed to Jesus, look at the fruit coming out of your life. Are you full of peace, joy, love, patience, and goodness? Do you have self control? Are you faithful? Are you gentle towards yourself and especially others? Probably not always because you're still human and on this side of heaven (I John 3:2) But is the genuine pattern of your life exhibiting these things? Disciples exude love. It oozes out of them toward everyone they encounter. When you've found that you were not gentle with someone and then did not exhibit self control in response to that, were you repentant and hopeful that you'll be more like Jesus next time? Did the love get clogged up? How can you get it flowing again?

Additionally, do you hear the word and do what it says? Do you let what you sense the Spirit is telling you as you read the bible, set you on a path toward Jesus or do you retreat into selfishness until you "understand more" or "are more comfortable" with what you sense you should do?

The ability to self evaluate like this, then change course and move forward toward love with a sense of joy and hope is what proves you're a disciple. Discipleship is taking ownership of the "fruit" you produce in your life with the help and power of the Holy Spirit. Discipleship is engaging the world you live in through the love of Christ now alive in you.

Discipleship is engaging the world you live in through the love of Christ now alive in you.

Remaining a Disciple

So, how do you keep moving forward? Well, use the practices you've learned about in this book with the purpose and outcome of staying connected to the vine. Staying connected to the vine? What the heck does that mean? John, one of Jesus' disciples, tells us that Jesus says "*I am the vine; you are the branches. If you remain in Me and I in you, you will bear much fruit; apart from Me you can do nothing.*" Remember, we just said our litmus test is whether or not we're bearing fruit. We can stay connected to Jesus by the practices throughout this book. But I also have an encouragement and a warning from Author Priscilla Shirer:

"If we want to produce fruit, we don't have to strive for it or sweat, or lose sleep, or grit our teeth in anxiety to achieve it.

The branch's only responsibility is to remain connected to the vine and REST there."

So take it easy. Rest in Jesus. Take these practices you've been introduced to in this book, one step at a time, one day at a time. Any progress is progress and remember - NOTHING can separate you from the love of Christ.

Paying it Forward

Guess what else? Discipleship is paying what you've discovered forward. Be constantly ready and look for opportunities to tell your story and give a reason for the hope you have whenever an opportunity presents itself. Look for opportunities to engage with all around you through the love of Christ in you. Do it in a way that relates and resonates with whomever you're sharing with. Don't sound pompous or churchy because that wouldn't be gentle, good and patient would it? - no matter how good your intentions are. Meet people where they're at just as Jesus would. I certainly hope Megan and I have done that for you with this book. If we haven't, would you PLEASE let us know? No joke. I wanna know. I wanna know because I'm always learning and growing as a follower of Christ - as a disciple of Christ and we're all in this together. Help me as I help you.

Jen's Coaching Questions:

1. How are you remaining in the vine and RESTING there?

2. What lingering questions do you have about discipleship? Write them down and take them to a Christ filled friend or pastor.

Before We Say Goodbye:

So, you live for Jesus now and you're daily moving forward in figuring out just what the heck that means. There is an enemy of your soul trying to derail you in these efforts. You can not overcome this enemy by sheer will power but if you focus your will power into these practices laid out in this book, the Holy Spirit will take it from there.

Additionally, I know we already addressed the importance of continual repentance, but let's also point out that in Acts 2 when Peter says to repent and be baptized, he's not saying confess every wrong thing you've ever done but rather to repent of the fact that you've been apart from Christ - you've been apart from love. That's it. So don't get frustrated over your failings. Just apologize for being apart from Christ, then use these practices to re attach to Him.

Thanks for being with us!

CPSIA information can be obtained
at www.ICGtesting.com
Printed in the USA
LVHW021537150722
723612LV00014B/1201

9 781633 572577